D0501028

Making Genes, Making Waves

B BECKWITH
Beckwith, Jonathan R.
Making genes, making waves

Making Genes, Making Waves

A SOCIAL ACTIVIST

IN SCIENCE

DISCARD

. . . . J O N

B E C K W I T H

HARVARD UNIVERSITY PRESS

CAMBRIDGE, MASSACHUSETTS

AND LONDON, ENGLAND 2002

Copyright © 2002 by Jon Beckwith

All rights reserved

Printed in the United States of America

Library of Congress Cataloging-in-Publication Data

Beckwith, Jonathan R.

    Making genes, making waves : a social activist in science /
Jon Beckwith.

      p. cm.

    Includes bibliographical references.

    ISBN 0-674-00928-2 (hardcover : alk. paper)

    1. Beckwith, Jonathan R.

  2. Geneticists—United States—Biography.

  3. Political activists—United States—Biography.

  4. Science—Social aspects.   I. Title.

QH429.2.B38 A3 2002

576.5′092—dc21

   [B]   2002022747

Designed by Gwen Nefsky Frankfeldt

▲ ▲ ▲

Contents

Making Genes, Making Waves

The Quail Farmer and the Scientist

The stone farmhouse surrounded by fields of rapeseed and wheat is unassuming. Yet enveloped within it is the story of a dramatic life. It is 1998 and I have come to this isolated spot to renew an old friendship, perhaps to find out something about myself, and certainly to explore a mystery. I am nervous about my meeting with Robert Williams—the first time we will have seen each other in thirty-five years. Since we were graduate students in the same biochemistry laboratory in the late 1950s, our lives have taken turns neither of us could have foreseen, Bob's being the most surprising. For while I have remained a scientist, Bob is now a quail farmer in Normandy.

▲ ▲ ▲ Bob Williams and I met when we started graduate school at Harvard University in 1957. He was far from his birthplace, Paris, where he grew up, the child of an American father and a French mother. I was only a few miles from home and just a mile from Mount Auburn Hospital in Cambridge, where I was born. Bob was enthusiastically committed to science. I was much less sure of my future, not having found the inspiration in science that I needed, and wondering what science had to do with real life. I was close to quitting in my first year as a chemistry graduate student when Bob suggested, "You should talk to Lowell Hager, my Ph.D. supervisor. I think you'd like working in his lab."

I made an appointment right away. A few days later, as I approached Professor Hager's office, I heard a series of sporadic clicks coming from inside, sounding like an erratic grandfather's clock. Puzzled, I waited a short time and then decided to knock. A voice said "come in," and as I entered, the source of the strange noise became clear. Lowell was standing in front of his desk, facing the door, with a Ping-Pong ball and paddle. The clicks were produced when the ball hit the door—Lowell was honing his skills for his next match.

In the Harvard of the 1950s, this casualness was unusual. Most of my professors were very formal, addressing me as "Mr. Beckwith," never as Jon, acting with what they considered to be the dignity appropriate to their position. Lowell's un-Harvard, unconstrained personality was a refreshing change and his lab was a relaxing place to work. It was clear that part of my lack of enthusiasm for science related to the work environments I had experienced in other labs—where students were driven to work long days and into the nights, so that their professors could add more papers to their bibliographies. Bob had been right. It took me very little time to decide that I wanted to do my Ph.D. with Lowell, switching from chemistry to biochemistry. So Bob and I ended up doing our Ph.D. work in the same lab for the next several years; without his suggestion I would probably no longer be in science.

Yet I was still not convinced that I was going to make a vocation of science. I looked at Bob and saw how committed he was to a scientific career, how he talked of nothing but science and did so with evident enthusiasm. He worked long hours in the lab apparently for the joy of it; there was no pressure from Lowell. He didn't seem to have a life outside of the lab. Could I make the same commitment? For those who knew us at the time, a bet on Bob rather than myself as the future scientist would have seemed a sure thing. Nevertheless, it was during my graduate years that I finally found the spark that carried me into my scientific career. The research papers of a group of French geneticists led by François Jacob and Jacques Monod at the Institut Pasteur in Paris overwhelmed me with the ingenuity of their genetic approaches, the clean logic that guided their experiments, and their elegant writing style. I was not a geneticist, but I now wanted to become one.

Bob and I finished our Ph.D.'s and set out on separate paths. I pursued my goal of working with my Parisian idols and began to learn bacterial genetics. I moved through several labs, traveling from Berkeley to Princeton, New Jersey, and then on to London and Cambridge, England. Several times, I asked François Jacob if there might be space for me in his laboratory; finally, in 1964, I was accepted and arrived at the Institut Pasteur for my last year of postdoctoral work. Meanwhile, Bob had spent a few years learning the genetics of bacterial viruses with Seymour Benzer at Purdue University and had then taken a position at the Institut de Biologie Physicochimique in Paris with Marianne Grunberg-Manago, a well-known biochemist.

I saw Bob once during this period, while my wife, Barbara, and I were living in England. One of my dreams, in addition to becoming a Pastorien (a researcher at the Institut Pasteur), was to own an old French car—the Citroen "traction avant" (front-wheel drive). This sleek black Citroen was as much the star of French gangster films of the forties and fifties as were Jean Gabin and Lino Ventura. Luckily, Bob's cousin in Paris ran a garage and had a used "traction avant." On a trip to Paris, Bob introduced Barbara and me to his cousin and we returned to England with the car of my dreams.

Bob and I did not see each other again for thirty-five years. I thought that we had little in common other than our involvement in science. And even in that realm, our specific interests had diverged. I still imagined that I might not be in science for the rest of my life. The friendship fostered by our close working relationship seemed to have ended.

▲ ▲ ▲ I hadn't thought much about Bob until late in the 1970s, when I visited Lowell Hager, who had moved to the University of Illinois at Urbana-Champaign. Lowell brought me up to date on Bob's life since I had last seen him. The story he told shattered my image of Bob and challenged my facile impression of a man totally immersed in science. In the late 1960s in Paris, Bob had married and moved into a commune, which surprised me. But after a year, the marriage soured and Bob's attitudes toward science also soured. He quit his laboratory research position, and ended up unemployed for some time.

The next events recounted by Lowell were even more startling and worrisome. In 1971, Bob moved to Chile with Sarah, the daughter from his marriage. Then governed by the Socialist Party of Salvador Allende, Chile sought international help to improve the nutrition and health of its poorest citizens. Bob started projects to find new sources of food in the seas that washed Chile's extensive coastline. Then, in 1973, came the violent military coup led by Augusto Pinochet. Not only were Chilean supporters of Allende tortured and murdered, but some foreigners who had helped the government were also targeted. The 1982 Costa-Gavras movie Missing presents the story of an American who suffered this fate. Neither Lowell nor Marianne had heard anything from Bob since the coup and feared that he was dead. Bob, at least as far as his scientific colleagues were concerned, had disappeared.

Here was a man who had seemed to me totally devoted to science and who rarely discussed political issues. How could he have changed so much—to reject science and plunge into such a deep political commitment?

▲ ▲ ▲ Perhaps if I had thought of the changes in my own life I might have considered more the parallels as well as the mirror images of the evolution of the two of us. I might have understood earlier what had led to the startling changes in Bob's life.

For at about the same time that Bob was leaving his laboratory for good, I was again beginning to have qualms about doing science, but this time for different reasons. My scientific career had taken off and I was now a professor and head of a research group at Harvard Medical School, but I was also beginning to worry seriously about the ways in which science could be misused. It was probably no coincidence that Bob and I were experiencing the same reservations about science. This was the late 1960s. The scientific community was not immune to the wider societal ferment.

In 1969, my laboratory group developed a technique for purifying a gene from the bacterium *Escherichia coli*. We became the first to totally separate a gene from all the other genes that normally surrounded it in the organism's chromosomes. We knew that having a purified gene sitting in a test tube in the laboratory would make possible a host of new experiments to reveal how genes work. We also recognized that our technique or its successors could be extended to isolate genes from organisms other than bacteria—even humans. I, along with several others in the lab, began to feel uneasy about our achievement; genetic engineering of humans might now be leaving the realm of science fiction. We knew that altering human genes could potentially provide health benefits; but we worried that a more likely use would be as a means of control and discrimination. Our fears arose at the time of the Vietnam War and the "high-tech battlefield"—the use of scientific developments such as the laser to pursue a war we opposed. It was a time of growing concern of many scientists that their work could be misused.

On the week that our paper on the gene isolation was to appear in *Nature* magazine, we called a press conference. We described our work and its scientific significance, and at the same time we issued a warning of the dangers we foresaw. Our press conference, which received international coverage, was to catalyze for me an examination of my own role in science. This event also led me into a career-long effort to inform both scientists and the public of the potential social impact of the new genetics.

The following year, 1970, I received the Eli Lilly Award of the American Society for Microbiology (ASM) for outstanding research contributions. I took the opportunity of the award speech at the annual ASM meeting to condemn the practices of the drug industry, of which the Eli Lilly Company was of course a representative. I then announced that I was donating the award money to a Black Panther Free Health Clinic and to a defense fund for thirteen Black Panther Party members who had been arrested in New York. The Panthers were the subject of particularly intense government repression at the time (see Chapter 4).

I became an activist in Science for the People, a radical group of scientists who sought to expose the ways in which science was used to destructive ends. I found myself deeply involved in public controversies over such projects as the attempt to find genetic links to criminal behavior and the popular presentation of sociobiology, a science that offers a genetic-evolutionary picture of human behavior and social arrangements. In the 1980s I visited Cuba to aid that country in its development of molecular biology. I have continued this activism to the present day. It has become integral to my life as a scientist.

▲ ▲ ▲ Finding Bob would eventually help me recognize how much we had in common. But finding him was made possible only by an extraordinary coincidence.

In 1984, I was still in science and still enthusiastic about it. A conference on a genetics topic close to my interests had been organized in the town of Concarneau in Brittany. After visiting friends in Paris, I boarded the train with a few colleagues for the several-hour ride to Concarneau. Hearing us speak English, a woman stopped to chat—a woman who was clearly of American background. Having discovered we were scientists, she mentioned that her brother had been a scientist. Then when she learned that we were at Harvard University, she told us that her brother was a graduate student in biochemistry at Harvard in the 1950's. "What was his name?" "Bob Williams!" I was stunned—first by the unlikely chance meeting, then, by the fearful realization that I was about to learn of his fate. "What happened to Bob? Everyone thinks that he was murdered during the Pinochet coup." She replied: "Oh no. He got out of Chile and is now a quail farmer in Normandy."

I asked Bob's sister for the address in Paris where his family still lived, thinking that some day I might visit Bob in Normandy. That was to take a while. My wife and I have traveled in France many times since then, but always, after a stop in Paris, we head south for bicycling in comfortable weather. The address remained unused in my Rolodex. However, in 1997, we decided to drop our prejudice against the colder, rainier northern weather and spend some time in Brittany and Normandy—and to see if we could track down Bob. I had begun to feel the need to reconnect with my past—family, friends, and places. Perhaps more comfortable with myself, I had gotten past the stage of rejecting that past.

I sent off a note to the old Parisian address, addressed to "La famille Williams," reminding the sister of our meeting in 1984, asking how we could reach Bob. Several months later, an envelope arrived with a business card inside. A picture of two quails was imprinted on one side next to the words "les Cailles de la Bichinière" (Bichinière quails). On the other side was a hand-written note: "We would be glad to see you (as long as we know ahead of time). I am now also maire [mayor] and have other local responsibilities which make me very busy."

▲ ▲ ▲ That is how, in June of 1998, Barbara and I found ourselves driving north from the house of friends in Brittany to the Normandy town of Céaucé, between Domfront and Mayenne. Bob was mayor of Céaucé, and La Bichinière was one of those clusters of houses in the countryside that affiliate with the nearby town, just as the farms of an earlier time had come under the sway of the local chateau.

Passing along a driveway, we entered a kind of courtyard surrounded by old stone houses on two sides and much newer and larger concrete buildings on the other two sides. The latter turned out to be where the quail are raised and then converted into various gourmet delicacies—quail eggs, quail paté, smoked quail legs, and deboned quail. A stout, very French-looking man stood by the driveway regarding us with a puzzled look as we drove in. Were we in the right place? I got out and approached the man hesitantly, but as soon as he started talking I knew that he was Bob.

"Call me François, that's how I'm known now." And I remembered from forty years earlier that his full name was François Robert Phillipe Williams. There was, at first, a kind of wariness between us—a wariness that perhaps is natural between people who have not seen each other for so long, but that also comes from some unspoken assumptions we held about each other. Our uneasiness quickly dissipated, however, as we got to know each other again. François introduced his wife, Dominique (he had remarried after returning from Chile), and his two children from this marriage, Marjorie and Kevin.

We went into the stone farmhouse, and François offered us a hard cider made from pears—a specialty of the Domfrontais region—with a little cassis added. Over this Normandy substitute for Kir, we began to fill in the thirty-five years that had seen so many changes. First, we learned of Bob's family background, filled with adventure I had never imagined. His father, whom I knew was the minister of an American church in Paris, had played an active political role before and during World War II. He had visited the United States many times during this period, lobbying for American entry into the war. He always returned with supplies for the French Resistance and aided refugees trying to escape the Nazis—until he was told by a sympathetic German officer in Portugal that he would be fusillé (shot by firing squad) if he returned to France again. Despite this warning, he did go back several times more, always in disguise. Finally he fled, taking his family to the United States.

Over the many years of trips to France, Barbara and I had ourselves become deeply absorbed by the history of the resistance movement in France during World War II and by the activities of those who had risked their lives to help Jews and others escape. We were especially taken with the story of the American Varian Fry. Operating out of Marseille, Fry had smuggled many people, including some prominent intellectuals and artists, out of Nazi-occupied France either by boat or across the Pyrénées. Like François's father, Fry had also been threatened with death. Among one of many connections we were to make, we discovered that both of our families had known Varian Fry. Fry had been a friend of my uncle when they were both at Harvard, and my parents had often played cards with the two of them during the 1930s. Not surprisingly, given their involvement in helping refugees, Fry and François's father had also been close friends.

We had visited the village of Le Chambon-sur-Lignon, where the Protestant pastor André Trocmé had convinced his parishioners to protect nearly five thousand Jewish refugees, mostly children. We had stopped at ten or more "Musées de la Résistance" and shrines to resistance heroes in our attempt to understand how people could behave so bravely under such dire conditions.

Then François told us of parallels between his father's experiences and his own in Chile. He was visiting his family in Paris when the Pinochet coup took place. In France he received messages from Chilean friends that he was on a death list and that the two places where he had lived had been burned down. Despite this mortal danger, he changed his appearance and used forged passports to return to Chile with supplies for those still resisting the new government. Then, also like his father, he was forced to give up these trips when the danger became too great, and he returned to Paris. Disillusioned by the destruction of all he had been able to accomplish in Chile, he decided to leave Paris and take up farming in Normandy, where the family of his new wife lived.

But, for me, there remained the question of why he had left science to begin with. François responded: "I really became convinced that science was being used in ways that were far more destructive than beneficial to people. I didn't see how I or a few scientists could do anything to stop these uses. The only path I could see was to quit science, so that, at least, I wouldn't be contributing to harmful social consequences."

I was surprised by this answer, because I didn't anticipate that the evolution of François's thinking would have so paralleled my own during the same period. I told François of my laboratory group's press conference in 1969, of the Eli Lilly Award and the Black Panthers, of my critiques of biological determinism and my visits to Cuba.

We were both elated to discover that, despite having made different choices, our political perspectives as well as our ideas about the role of science in society had evolved in much the same way. Over the weekend, each of us would occasionally burst out with excitement at yet some other indication of this new-found connection. The wariness was gone. Ironically, our initial cautious interactions came about because of my image of François as the narrow scientist, and because of François's knowledge that I had stayed in science. I never imagined the extent of his political activism or the reasons for his disillusionment with science. And from his side, could he really trust someone who, as far as he knew, had blithely continued to produce science with its inherent dangers? Now, after our discussions, he had come to the point of wondering, "If I had realized what it was possible to do within science about these issues, I might have stayed."

▲ ▲ ▲ François took us on a tour of Céaucé. Although he had been disillusioned by his Chilean experience, he did feel that here it was still possible to have some impact as an activist at the local level. He told us how he had assumed the mayorship of a town that was deteriorating as industry left and the townspeople and farmers fled for the big cities. Both by luring small industry to Céaucé and by vastly improving the amenities (adding senior housing, sports facilities, a campground, a park with trails and a fishing pond), he reversed the downward trend. His success had led to his election as head of the mayors' organization of the Domfrontais region.

Back at La Bichinière, François led us through the two farm buildings, showing us how he raised his quail. When he first arrived in Normandy, the other quail farmers were loath to reveal the secrets of their trade. François felt that, despite his misgivings about science, his scientific training helped him to think better about the techniques that would be most successful. The last day of our stay we were treated to an all-quail meal.

▲ ▲ ▲ There are lots of questions, political and personal, that I have asked of myself since our meeting. Why did I know so little of François's background even though we worked practically side by side for three years? Had I overstated the effect that people like my-self could have by staying in science and speaking out on issues of science and society? Had one of us made the better choice or were they both good choices?

The meeting at La Bichinière and these afterthoughts have strengthened my enthusiasm for putting together this book. It is about how my enchantment with science grew and how that enchantment was paralleled by a growing concern about the consequences of science. It is about a period when social activism was almost the norm in science. It is about changes in my social and personal assumptions. It is about some of the issues that I feel geneticists must confront in thinking about the impact of their work on society. It is about the role of scientists in society and their relationship with the nonscientific world.

CHAPTER 2

Becoming a Scientist

How does one become a scientist? Perhaps the most common image is the high school student who spends afternoons at home playing with a chemistry set, dissecting a frog, or visiting museums to marvel at dinosaur bones. Many well-known scientists began this way. Stephen Jay Gould, the renowned paleontologist (and social critic of science), places the origins of his scientific career in trips with his father to New York's Museum of Natural History. In contrast, my former colleague James Shapiro, an English major in college, was inspired by a genetics course he took as a senior, shifted gears, and went off to graduate school in biology. One of the founders of molecular biology, Gunther Stent, claims in his autobiography that he became a scientist to "get the girls." Neither a life-long devotee of science nor inspired to pursue science by a sudden epiphany and never imagining that scientists were particularly attractive to women, I became a committed scientist by a slow process, full of hesitation and uncertainty.

In high school, I excelled at math and chemistry, thriving on the solution of mathematical puzzles and the comparable thinking involved in understanding the reactions of chemical elements and compounds. But there were no chemistry set explosions, no frog remains, no dusty museums, no displays at science fairs. In fact, the classes I remember most vividly are my English and French classes. Taught by two strong women, Miss Leathers and Miss Miles, these classes instilled in me a life-long love of writing and of the French language.

At Harvard College, again I got my best grades in science and switched my major from math to chemistry. Advanced mathematics appeared too abstract to me and too distant from life. Chemistry dealt mostly with compounds and molecules found in the real world—in plants, in us, in chemical factories. Yet the pull of the humanities was still very strong. In college, I was most influenced by Albert J. Guerard's comparative literature course, where I was introduced to the books of Gide, Camus, and Kafka, first heard of Dada and Surrealism, and learned of more obscure novelists such as John Hawkes and Djuna Barnes. Science was puzzle solving—figuring out mathematical proofs or devising pathways for the synthesis of complex organic compounds—it was fun. Literature in the hands of Guerard seemed connected with living a life. I became fascinated by the literature produced in the southern United States, after reading Faulkner's *Absalom, Absalom*. I amassed a collection of the fiction of southern writers going back to the mid-nineteenth century. Maybe I would change careers.

But science was what I was best at. I took the path of least resistance when I finished college: graduate school in science—I was accepted into the Ph.D. program in chemistry at Harvard. During the summer after college graduation, I bicycled alone through Europe to visit with my girl friend (wife-to-be), Barbara, who was living for the summer with a family in Turin. This trip was most notable for me because it included my first visit to Paris. In Paris, my loneliness and despair at traveling by myself disappeared in the lights, liveliness, and beauty of the city. I now had two loves.

I returned to Cambridge in the fall of 1957 to start graduate school in chemistry at Harvard. It was then that the full realization of what I had chosen hit me. I was taking only chemistry courses, and was no longer exposed to the broader world of ideas. My colleagues were now all scientists, most of whom were totally focused on their work and had few outside interests. I felt ever more strongly the need for a connection between my daily work and the outside world. I was seriously thinking of dropping out of graduate school. It was then that Bob Williams entered my life. He provided at least a temporary block to my slide out of science when he suggested I talk to Lowell Hager.

I was happy working in Lowell's lab; I still found pleasure in solving puzzles—part of the daily work of a biologist. Also, I was now part of a small group that worked together, a social unit that partied together, gossiped about the other labs, and went out to play golf—Lowell's favorite hobby along with Ping-Pong. Although I was still in the Chemistry Department, I was now doing biochemical research—as I saw it, another step closer to real life. I was studying in my courses how organisms from bacteria to humans manage to live and grow. In the laboratory, I was growing a living organism; my project was to find out how a fungus found in hothouses could incorporate chloride atoms into the organic compounds that it made. This was a typical basic research project in biochemistry of that era: working out the biochemical pathways for all sorts of processes and organisms. My fungus, which daily spread its black mass over the growth media in my flasks, was more alive than any mathematical and chemical formula on a page. But it did not replace for me the ideas and the social ferment that I had been exposed to in college. My real excitement still bubbled up when I thought or talked about worlds other than the scientific world. I audited a course taught by the sociologist David Riesman and one by the visiting professor Alan Tate on literature of the South.

Chemistry was then a field with a strong conservative streak. Not only was there a fairly rigid view of what path one should take to be a chemist, but the social and political environment in chemistry departments was confining. The field seemed to have retained much of its authoritarian German roots. Biochemistry was more welcoming to me, although the origins of many of its practitioners in the field of chemistry made it only a slight improvement. It was during my graduate career that the emergence of the new field of molecular biology began to dramatically revolutionize sensibilities and the climate in the life sciences.

Molecular biology was anointed as a scientific discipline in the late 1950s, formed from a gathering of scientists in the disparate fields of genetics, biochemistry, and biophysics. Its roots go back to the entry of a number of young physicists into biology in the 1940s. These pioneers, convinced that the fundamental problems in physics had been solved, sought new scientific principles in the study of living organisms. I was only vaguely conscious of these changes that had been taking place in biology. Trained in the very separate discipline of chemistry, I had not heard of the discovery of the structure of DNA (deoxyribonucleic acid) by James Watson and Francis Crick in 1953. At first, I was not even aware that Jim Watson was a professor in the nearby Biological Laboratories.

Not only did Jim Watson play a major scientific role in this revolution, but he probably also contributed in important ways to the cultural revolution in science that molecular biology brought with it. Iconoclastic, unchemist-like, outspoken in his contempt for older-line scientists or, for that matter, pretty much anyone who was not part of "the club," he was easy to spot in Cambridge in his bright red sports car and famous for throwing dancing parties, all at the same time continuing his brilliant career. He made the idea of being a scientist and having an outside life seem like a real possibility. The flood of funding from the U.S. government that came into science after the Russians' launch of Sputnik in 1957 had resulted in a large cohort of young scientists entering biology as well as other fields. It may well have been the new scientific culture represented by Watson that contributed to the entry of a different breed of young scientist into the field of molecular biology.

The change in sensibilities that molecular biology brought with it made being in science more congenial for me. More important, a microbiology course taught by Jim Watson and William Sistrom provided me with the needed inspiration. It wasn't the course content or the lectures—Jim was almost incomprehensible, with his stream-of-consciousness rambling. Rather, it was burying myself in the Biology Department library to prepare a research paper for the course. I read a few background articles published in the obscure (to me) journal *Comptes Rendus de l'Académie des Sciences Françaises* (*Proceedings of the French Academy of Sciences*). The lead authors were François Jacob, Elie Wollman, and Jacques Monod, all researchers at the Institut Pasteur in Paris. They were using bacterial genetics to solve very basic problems of biology. Their papers were a revelation to me. A style of doing science new to me—daring leaps of logic, simple experiments that seemed to yield profound insights—the papers were not written in the dry scientific language I was used to, but came alive with elegant rhetorical strokes that persuaded. I had never imagined science being like this—almost literary, artistic, and scientific at the same time. I sought every article these authors had written, going through years of back issues of the *Comptes Rendus* and the *Annales de l'Institut Pasteur*, reading about scientific issues that had nothing to do with my research paper. Without my strong high school training in French, I might never have come upon this important inspiration.

I now became obsessed with the goal of working with my idols at the Institut Pasteur in Paris. It didn't hurt that the institute was in Paris, the city I had fallen in love with in the summer of 1957. I was no longer following the path of least resistance—I was going to follow my inspiration. I was no longer doing science because I was good at it or because it was just fun—I now found that I loved what science could be. I wrote to Jacob inquiring about a postdoctoral position. I spoke to him during his visit to Harvard in 1959. He had no space for me and suggested that I first learn some genetics in the laboratory of Arthur Pardee, then at the University of California at Berkeley.

Arthur Pardee had worked with Jacob and Monod during the previous year and together they had published one of the classic papers in biology. The three scientists had been studying how the bacterium *Escherichia coli* went about using the milk sugar lactose for growth. The bacteria produced two proteins for this purpose: (1) a transport protein located in the cell's membrane that took the lactose from the growth medium and concentrated it inside the bacterial cell; and (2) an enzyme, β-galactosidase, which broke down lactose into two smaller sugars that the bacteria were more readily able to digest. The two proteins were encoded by two genes in a region of the bacterial chromosome they called the lac region. "Intelligently," the bacteria had a mechanism to ensure that these two proteins were only made when the bacteria were exposed to lactose in their environment. They did not waste their energy making the proteins when a sugar other than lactose was in their growth media. Using a combination of genetics and physiological studies with the bacteria, Pardee, Jacob, and Monod obtained convincing evidence that when lactose was not present, a molecule called a repressor "repressed" the genes that had the information for making β-galactosidase and the transport protein. The repressor prevented the genes from making these products. But when lactose was added to the growth media, small amounts of the sugar entered the bacterial cells and inactivated the repressor. Then the genes, no longer being repressed, were able to make the required proteins, thus allowing the bacteria to digest the lactose.

The paper published by Pardee, Jacob, and Monod on this work —abbreviated the PaJaMo paper at the time—is considered one of a handful of conceptual papers that underlie all of what is done in molecular biology today. Understanding that genes could be turned on and off and that specific molecules such as repressors (proteins as it later turned out) could exert this kind of regulation became fundamental to the study of many biological problems. These included development of complex organisms such as humans, the change from a normal cell into a cancerous one, and the methods by which organisms manage to survive various challenges from the environment.

I accepted Jacob's suggestion that I first go to work with Arthur Pardee. I finished my Ph.D. thesis with Lowell Hager in December of 1960 and immediately drove across the country with Barbara to Berkeley, California. We had married that month at Barbara's parents' house in Pennsylvania. I would begin my work in Pardee's lab and Barbara would continue her job as an English teacher in the Berkeley schools. Just as Berkeley in 1960 was very different from Cambridge, Arthur Pardee was a contrast to Lowell Hager. Art was so shy in some ways that he did not even look at his students while lecturing to a class. He was and is, nevertheless, a remarkable and prolific scientist. He had been involved in a host of important findings that opened up new areas of study in the burgeoning field of molecular biology. These included discovering the cellular machinery (ribosomes) required to make proteins, understanding how chemicals can act as mutagens, and deducing an important mechanism for the control of metabolism in living cells (feedback inhibition). Many scientists, having made just one of these seminal findings, would have spent the rest of their careers working out the details of what they had started. And in fact, Lowell Hager has successfully continued to this day the work on chloride metabolism that we began in his lab back in the late 1950s. But Art was too restless to be content with that. He regularly moved on to new areas, often following up unusual findings that had emerged from an earlier experiment. I began to understand that being a scientist did not mean adhering to a rigid set of rules, but that people with very different personalities could follow very different paths with equal degrees of success.

Despite his shyness and the uniqueness of his own career, Art had strong feelings about what was required for success in science. He didn't hesitate to express these to his students and postdoctoral fellows. Shortly after I arrived in the lab, a student of Art's had just returned from a trip to Cuba. Art, disturbed by the student's extra-curricular activities, called her into his office and gave her what we came to call "the balloon lecture." As the student recounted it, Pardee's lecture went something like this: "Scientists are like balloons. They begin with a certain amount of ballast-sandbags [trips to Cuba in this student's case]. If they are going to be successful in their ascent, they have to throw off the sandbags or they will never rise." And then, as an afterthought: "Of course, there are some balloons that never rise no matter how many sandbags they throw off."

I began to fear getting the same lecture. I was having a problem pursuing that success or perhaps developing the needed desire for it. My lab bench was located on the fourth floor of the Virus Laboratories, high up on the Berkeley campus—from my window I could see the whole campus, Berkeley, San Francisco, its bay and the Golden Gate Bridge. The weather seemed unceasingly sunny and the campus was alive with activity. I would leave the lab at lunchtime and stop to hear speakers in Sproul Plaza denouncing U.S. policy at home and abroad. I did not foresee that this contrast with the political passivity of Cambridge was a harbinger of the profound social upheavals that would become so prominent later in the 1960s. I ate lunch outdoors with friends, talked about these changes, sometimes even played tennis at the Rose Gardens, and, frequently, did not return to the lab again that day. One of these friends, John Leonard (now a major literary critic), got me a gig reading from Sean O'Casey's autobiography over the Pacifica radio station, KPFA. Again, doubts began to seep in about my future as a scientist.

But an unexpected change in my situation was to remove the temptations of Berkeley from my life and stem these doubts. Just as my discovery of the Comptes Rendus papers had provided me with the inspiration to be a scientist, news from Art Pardee was to allow me to fulfill that inspiration. Only a few months after arriving in Berkeley, Art called his group together to announce that he had accepted a job in the Biology Department at Princeton University and that we were welcome to move with him or we could find another lab at Berkeley to work in. Although I considered moving to the lab of Gunther Stent, another bacterial geneticist at Berkeley, the work in Art's lab suited me best. Also, my best hope of getting to the Institut Pasteur ultimately was to continue working with Art. I, along with most of his group, moved to Princeton, New Jersey, in the summer of 1961.

If Cambridge and Berkeley had seemed dramatically different, the contrast between Berkeley and Princeton was even starker. Princeton was a small community centered on the university, which itself seemed very ingrown: largely an undergraduate institution with much of its life focused on the student clubs and conservative, even reactionary—many student dormitory windows were still adorned with Confederate flags. This most southern-oriented of the Ivy League schools attracted students from elite families of the South. Here there were no distractions, as there were in Berkeley. There was little to do but work in the lab—a five-minute walk from our apartment.

Work and read and think. I worked longer hours in the lab than I ever had. I spent more time in the library, educating myself in ge-

genes into a ribonucleic acid (RNA) transcript began at this point. Art and I obtained these mutant bacteria from Jacob and used them to produce new classes of mutations that affected the ability of the cell to use lactose. As I studied these mutations in depth both at Princeton and in London, it became clear to me that the mutations obtained by the Pasteur group could not be in the lac promoter, the site for initiation of RNA transcription; their claim to have defined a promoter site was incorrect. Rather, the mutations were within the gene for β-galactosidase and interfered with the making of the protein. They did this by interrupting the translation of the RNA transcript of the gene. The feature of the Jacob-Monod model that I had disproved was, in some senses, a detail. Nevertheless, rather than working with Jacob, I had ended up disproving one aspect of his work.

Somehow, toppling giants—showing that such great scientists could make a mistake—was almost as exciting to people in the field as discovering a new fundamental biological fact. Suddenly, I was perceived as an iconoclast. Invitations started to pour in to present my work at meetings. Instead of having no prospects for a job in the United States, I was now being considered for faculty positions at both the Harvard Medical School and the University of California at Berkeley. Bernard Davis, chair of the Department of Bacteriology and Immunology at the Harvard Medical School, came over to London to interview me for the position there. Sydney Brenner, another one on my list of most admired scientists, came down to London from Cambridge, England, to ask if we could collaborate on a project with some of my mutants, and to offer me a postdoctoral place in his lab. And finally, my dream came true, François Jacob responded positively to my third request to work in his lab, perhaps interested in welcoming a challenger. With these invitations in hand, I was able to land a fellowship to support myself in my final postdoctoral years. And an offer arrived for the job at Harvard. As other scientists learned of my findings, I had been transformed from a nonperson to a person in the world of biology.

So the year in London ended up being a very good one. It was also good for Barbara and me personally as we became very close friends with John Scaife. John and I worked right next to each other at Hammersmith Hospital. He had come from a working-class area of Leeds, where his choice to go to university had been seen as a betrayal of his class. John was no longer welcome in the neighborhood where he had grown up. He was also gay and he anguished over his situation in an England that appeared to be little changed since the days of Oscar Wilde. Before I left London, I invited John to join me when I set up my laboratory at the Harvard Medical School.

In December of 1963, I moved up to Cambridge, England, to work with Sydney Brenner for nine months. Jacob would not have space until the fall of 1964. In Cambridge, I got a sense of the atmosphere that Jim Watson was to write about several years later in his memoir *The Double Helix*. The Medical Research Council institute on Hills Road was packed with Nobel Prize winners and Nobel Prize winners-to-be—Francis Crick, Max Perutz, John Kendrew, and Fred Sanger. Many, including me, feel that Sydney Brenner should have been in that category. Every day was an intense intellectual experience, particularly the inevitable British teatime, when we hashed out scientific ideas together. Every day I was also exposed to the extraordinary arrogance and superciliousness that invested the social as well as the scientific life at Cambridge. There were only a few scientists outside the Cambridge circle considered worthy of respect by these Cantabridgians, who were adept at repartee. They used their rapier-sharp wit to ridicule most other scientists around the world. At one of the teas, Francis Crick read to us from a letter he had sent to an American geneticist who had complained about the failure of Brenner and Crick to credit his work in a recent paper. The letter patronized the aggrieved scientist in caustic phrases that were obviously meant to wound. The teatimes at Hammersmith had been like real tea parties compared to the same events at Cambridge.

Nevertheless, working closely with Sydney Brenner became the formative experience of my scientific career. He came to the lab earlier than everyone else, looked at the agar plates on which my bacteria were growing, and was ready to interpret the results for me by the time I arrived in the lab. He discussed our work and that of others practically nonstop. Each day at the lab left me exhausted but exhilarated. The intensity of spending so much time with Sydney, mostly just listening to him and appreciating his approach to biological questions—his profound belief in the power of genetics as a tool for understanding nature—was like being brainwashed, but in a good sense. I became even more of a believer than I had been. When Sydney suggested that I stay another year instead of going to Jacob's lab, I demurred. I had my powerful dream of living in Paris, but also I had to escape this intensity and make sure that I could think for myself again. I was also a bit disgusted by the superior attitude in Cambridge, which I had had enough of as an undergraduate at Harvard.

As in London, in Cambridge I made a friendship that was to prove important for my scientific career. Working in the same lab and collaborating with me was Ethan Signer, an American who had recently finished his Ph.D. at MIT. Ethan was one of the new breed of molecular biologists who helped break the mold of staidness that permeated its precursor field, biochemistry. Back in the States, he had played fiddle and sung folk music with a blue-grass group, the Charles River Valley Boys. In 1963, he cut a record with Richie Farina, Eric von Schmidt, and Bob Dylan (playing under a pseudonym). Like me, Ethan had doubts about his career in science. Like me, he desperately sought to be accepted into the lab of François Jacob and finally succeeded. Together, we went to Paris, and ended up sharing a lab at the Institut Pasteur.

Paris was everything I could have hoped for scientifically. I did not have the close relationship with François Jacob that I had experienced with Sydney Brenner, but that was all right because I was at a point where I needed to be more independent. Both Jacob and Monod were very different from scientists I had encountered in England and the United States. They had already seemed larger than life to me because of their scientific style, a style that I came to identify more and more with French culture. Their writings were articulate and elegant; they persuaded with seductive logic. At daily lunches with Jacob, Monod, Wollmann, the equally eminent André Lwoff, and their students, I was continually exposed to their philosophy of science. I became an even more passionate convert to their religion—to their belief in simplicity and beauty as guiding principles in experiments and theory. As Monod had put it, "A beautiful model or theory may not be right, but an ugly one must be wrong." (While colleagues have cited Monod as the source of this quotation, he was no doubt aware that similar sentiments had been previously attributed to Paul Dirac and Thomas H. Huxley.)

My awe increased as I learned more of the personal histories of Jacob and Monod. Both were imposing figures, Jacob tall and graceful, Monod smaller but ruggedly attractive. A French Jew, Jacob had escaped from France during World War II and gone to England to join the Free French forces of Charles De Gaulle. Later, he was badly wounded during the invasion that was to liberate France. At the same time, the French Huguenot Monod, while holding a research position at the Institut Pasteur, worked secretly with the French Resistance in Paris. After the war, Monod became involved in a group that Albert Camus had organized to consider leftist alternatives to Communism. (A well-known photograph from a later time shows Monod assisting wounded students at the barricades during the May 1968 student uprising.) I had become accustomed to sidewalk radical orators in Berkeley, but now, for the first time, I was meeting leading scientists with progressive political positions. I had come a long way from the Chemistry Department at Harvard, and in only a few short years.

In the story of my scientific career, the stay in the Institut Pasteur is particularly important for a discovery that Ethan Signer and I made. I had begun to follow up on some studies by Jacob and his student François Cuzin. They had found a means of moving—of transposing—the genes (lac) responsible for lactose utilization from their normal position on the E. coli chromosome to other positions on that same chromosome. I decided to generate a new collection of these "transposition" strains, each of which would have the lac genes moved to a different place on the bacterial chromosome. I noticed that one of the transposition strains I obtained now had the lac genes moved close to a spot on the chromosome where a bacterial virus called $\phi80$ tended to insert its own chromosome. Virus $\phi80$ could either kill E. coli cells or go dormant by recombining its genetic material into the bacterial chromosome. The dormancy could be overcome by treating the bacteria with low doses of ultraviolet light, which caused the viral DNA to excise from the chromosome; the virus then multiplied and killed the cell. Sometimes when $\phi80$ excised, it would bring with it neighboring chromosomal genes. These bacterial genes then became a part of the virus chromosome.

By coincidence, Ethan, working right next to me, was studying the $\phi80$ virus, so I mentioned my finding to him. He suggested that since, in the particular transposition strain I had isolated, the lac genes were adjacent to the site of insertion of $\phi80$, we might be able to get the virus to incorporate the nearby lac genes into its own chromosome when it exited from the bacterial chromosome.

We took my strain, obtained a derivative of it with the $\phi80$ chromosome integrated near the lac genes, and treated the bacterial cells with low doses of ultraviolet light. Among the virus particles that emerged from the bacteria after killing them were a small number that now carried the lac genes in addition to their own genetic material. (See Figure 1.)

Ethan's idea had worked. We had incorporated the lac genes into the virus's chromosome, a much smaller chromosome than that of the bacteria. These genes were now separated from the rest of the bacteria's chromosomal genes. This would make the detailed study of how these genes work much simpler. However, this technique could not be generalized; our success was due to my chance finding of a lac transposition that just happened to be close to the chromosomal site where the $\phi80$ virus inserted its DNA. So, I then conceived of a way in which we could direct the lac genes specifically to go to this part of the bacterial chromosome. When this approach succeeded, we realized that we had developed a general means of incorporating bacterial genes into viruses.

This was the first time anyone had developed a method for taking genes out of their normal chromosomal position and putting them into small pieces of DNA (viral DNA) that were easy to manipulate and study. This general approach eventually came to be known as cloning. While later techniques for cloning would vastly improve over our own, we had set the precedent conceptually for the way to study genes and their function. This last discovery highlighted a productive scientific year at the Institut Pasteur that included collaborations with two other American postdoctoral fellows, Austin Newton and Wolf Epstein.

In the fall of 1965, I returned to my new position at the Harvard Medical School in Boston and set up my lab to continue some of the work I had begun in Europe. I was happy and lucky to have John Scaife join me as a postdoctoral fellow, both because of our

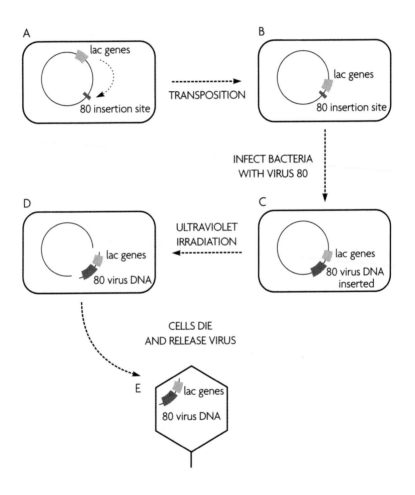

A

lac genes

80 insertion site

TRANSPOSITION

B

lac genes

80 insertion site

INFECT BACTERIA
WITH VIRUS 80

D

lac genes

80 virus DNA

ULTRAVIOLET
IRRADIATION

C

lac genes

80 virus DNA
inserted

CELLS DIE
AND RELEASE VIRUS

E

lac genes

80 virus DNA

friendship and because of our already productive working relationship. Along with a technician, Neil Krieger, we initiated a project to follow up on my earlier finding that the so-called promoter mutations that Jacob and his colleagues had isolated were not, in fact, in a promoter site. We wanted to devise a way to obtain real promoter mutations. We would look for mutational changes in the lac genes that would prevent the cell from ever recognizing the lac genes as genes that should be expressed. The genes would be permanently and forever repressed. If we could find these, we would then begin to study how this site works.

The problem in looking for such mutations was that all kinds of changes in these genes could prevent the cells from metabolizing lactose. I didn't want to make the same mistake that Jacob and Monod had made and choose the wrong set of mutations. I finally came up with an idea for finding mutations in this promoter site that would behave very differently from any other kinds that interfered with lactose metabolism. Rather than seeking mutant strains where the cells were completely unable to use lactose for growth, we would look for those in which the rate at which lactose was used was greatly reduced but was not nil. We predicted that if these

Figure 1 *(facing page).* Cloning of the lac genes into the chromosome of a virus. A: Diagram of an *E. coli* cell with its single circular chromosome. B: Through a series of steps not shown here, we move (transpose) the lac genes from their normal position on the chromosome to a position near the site where the DNA of the ϕ80 virus inserts into the bacterial chromosome. C: After the bacteria are infected with the virus, the virus's DNA inserts into the bacterial chromosome. D: Upon ultraviolet irradiation of the bacteria, the ϕ80 DNA excises from the bacterial chromosome, sometimes carrying the nearby lac genes with it. The ultraviolet irradiation has also caused the virus DNA to start a cycle of virus production that kills the bacterial cell. E: One of the few viruses coming out of the dead bacteria that now carry the lac genes along with their own DNA. The DNA of the virus is surrounded by the virus's protein coat.

"leaky" mutations were in a promoter region, they should reduce the amounts of both of the lac proteins, β-galactosidase and the transport protein. The idea worked beautifully. The mutants we picked out as having these special properties were exactly what we had hoped for. We had found the first mutants in a promoter site for a gene. Our subsequent work with these mutations helped us define many aspects of how this site works.

We also continued the work I had started with Ethan Signer in Paris. We had shown that it was possible to "clone" the lac genes into a particular virus's genome, and now two postdoctoral fellows in my lab, Karen Ippen and Jim Shapiro, went on to clone lac into another virus called λ. And Susan Gottesman, a graduate student, found that we could carry out the same procedure with other genes from the bacterial chromosome.

Then, insight struck. One day early in 1969, I was drawing the structure of two of the viruses carrying the lac genes on a piece of paper. Suddenly, it hit me. The chromosomes of the two viruses of this pair were largely composed of different DNA sequences. They shared only the gene for β-galactosidase. I saw that these two viruses might be used to completely purify this lac gene. We should be able to separate the two strands of DNA of each of these viruses, mix all of the strands together and cause them to pair randomly with each other. This procedure should lead to some structures in which a double-stranded lac gene would form between strands from the two viruses. These structures ought to have much of the rest of their DNA unpaired—single-stranded—because the DNA came from different viruses with different sequences. By treating this DNA with a particular enzyme, a DNAase that attacked only single-stranded DNA, we should be able to destroy all single-stranded regions, leaving only the double-stranded region that was the lac gene. That gene would be pure. Our task was made much easier by a very clever variation on this initial idea suggested to us by Garrett Ihler, a postdoctoral fellow in a nearby lab. If these ideas worked, we would be the first ever to purify a gene. For our own research and that of others, a purified gene would immeasurably simplify the study of gene expression and regulation.

Everyone in the lab was excited. Jim Shapiro offered to test out the idea for gene purification and within a short time believed that he had the process working. To verify that we had what we hoped for, we would have to visualize the gene by some form of microscopy. We recruited Lorne MacHattie, an electron microscopist, to see if our gene could be observed with the very powerful electron microscope. The very next day after passing the material to Lorne, he called us over to take a look through the microscope lens. What we saw was a string of DNA exactly of the length predicted for the lac gene encoding β-galactosidase (see Figure 2). It was unquestionably beautiful to us, but I suppose it really looked more like a worm than anything else.

It always seems like a little miracle when something works in my experiments. But because of what this molecule was, this was a big miracle. We were pioneers, the first to look at an individual gene. This is one of the joys of doing science—the pleasure of knowing that one is the first to have discovered a new fact, to have obtained a new molecule, or even just to have had a new idea.

We had done these experiments both because we recognized that the isolation of a pure gene would be considered a significant genetic accomplishment and because the gene could be useful for biological studies. Although much had been deduced already about the function of genes from working with live bacteria, a detailed understanding could only come from a combination of these in vivo experiments with studies of the very DNA of the gene in the test tube.

As we prepared to send a paper on this work off to the journal *Nature*, we were aware that this achievement would probably re-

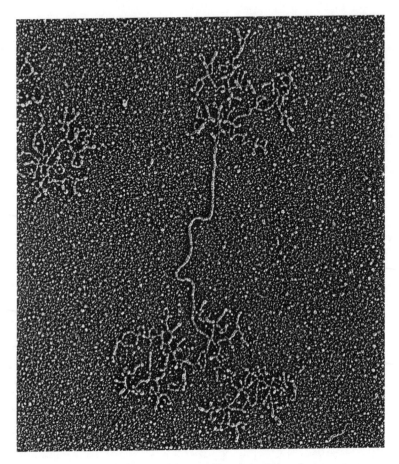

Figure 2. Purifying the lac gene (photographs taken with an electron microscope). As described in the text, we obtained two different viruses that carried the lac genes in their DNA. (See Figure 1 on page 30 for the origin of one of these, φ80lac.) We separated the double-stranded DNA molecules of the two viruses into single strands by incubating the DNA at high temperature (termed "melting" the DNA). We mixed together samples of one of the single DNA strands from one virus with one of the other virus and caused them to reform a double-stranded molecule again. The only regions of the DNA that can form double-stranded DNA are portions of the lac genes. These electron micrographs

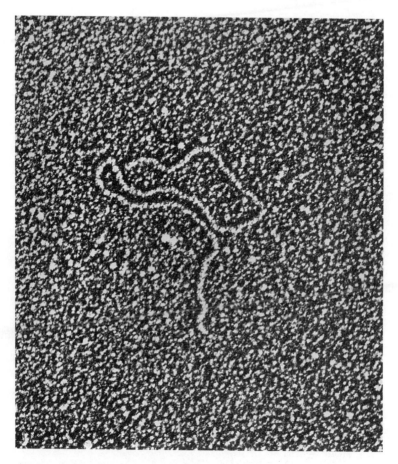

show DNA molecules. Left: Here a structure appears in in which a central part over a certain length is thicker than the rest (double-stranded). At both ends of this thicker region, two thinner strands can be seen. Right: After treatment of the DNA molecules seen on the left with an enzyme that will destroy only single-stranded DNA, only the thicker (double-stranded) piece of DNA remains. Because of the particular structures of the two virus DNA molecules, this piece of DNA contains only one of the lac genes, that encoding the enzyme β-galactosidase.

ceive public attention. With the steps we had used, it was not a stretch of the imagination to propose that any gene from E. coli could be purified. Suddenly, the possibility of extracting specific genes from other organisms, including humans, did not seem so far-fetched. With that prospect on the horizon, we began to imagine the uses of such gene manipulation. Medical researchers had begun to think about how to translate new knowledge in molecular biology into cures for genetic diseases. Some proposed that introducing genes into humans who suffered from specific genetic defects—gene therapy—might compensate for the defective gene and reverse the course of the disease. However, without purified genes in hand, this approach seemed far off. Now, we thought, our achievement made the concept of gene therapy seem more realistic. If gene therapy efforts were successful, wouldn't some people go beyond the treatment of genetic diseases to change other human characteristics by such techniques? Who would be in charge of these techniques? Who would decide what genes should be changed? How would the application of genetic manipulation—genetic engineering—to humans be controlled? Should we worry that governments might even impose genetic engineering programs that achieved the same ends as those outlined in Aldous Huxley's Brave New World? Should we really be going down this road?

I, along with two of my coauthors, Jim Shapiro and Larry Eron (a medical student), called a press conference during the week that our paper was published. We described our genetic feat, the first isolation of a gene from a chromosome. We also admitted to our fears. "We have no right to pat ourselves on the back," we announced. We stated that such gene manipulations could ultimately hold dangers for humanity. The next day, newspaper headlines warned of the imminent creation of new Frankenstein's monsters. The coverage was international. The reporters obviously regarded our accomplishment as a breakthrough, but also, because of our warning, as a threat.

What led me, along with some of my coworkers, all of us ambitious young molecular biologists, to send such a mixed message about science to the public? I had never before participated in any effort to link scientific research with its possible misuse. Little in my scientific career up to that point had connected with social concerns about science. But just as there was a scientific trajectory in the late 1950s and 1960s, there was also a political trajectory. The next chapter describes this latter trajectory and how the two joined in the fateful press conference. The rest of the book shows how this union of the scientific and the political affected the rest of my career.

Becoming an Activist

The press conference my colleagues and I called in 1969 was a catalyst that would join together two separate strands of my life, the scientific and the political—much as my discovery of the French papers of the Pasteur group in the late 1950s had melded my involvement in science with my enthusiasm for the literary, the intuitional. Until the press conference, I had never thought very deeply about the social consequences of scientific research. I do remember that my high school chemistry teacher, Jack Hall, forcefully emphasized the military applications of science. He started off a class by asking us a question about one of the elements in the periodic table. One day he challenged us to tell him what titanium was used for. Silence—no one knew. Mr. Hall's face turned red, and he bellowed at us: "Our boys are dying over Korea in jet planes made of titanium and you can't tell me what titanium is used for!" We had to squat on the floor for five minutes, his favorite punishment for a display of ignorance.

Of all the science courses I took in high school, college, and graduate school, Jack Hall's was the only one in which I heard of any connections between science and its social implications. Nothing in my training as a scientist could explain my choice to call the press conference. Instead, it is easier to see this decision arising out of my growing political radicalization in the 1950s and 1960s. Seeing the world in more political ways prepared me to think about science in its social context.

The origins of any political being must be complex; I will try to unravel the strands of my own story. As with the evolution of my scientific career, there was no epiphany that transformed me. Nor did I grow up in a left-wing family like many I came to know. Although my parents subscribed to some left-wing journals, such as the newspaper PM and I. F. Stone's newsletter, they were liberal Democrats. My uncle, Allan Rosenberg, a lawyer in Boston, was called up before a congressional committee investigating Communists, and, as a result, lost most of his clients. While I was aware of this—one article on that hearing appeared in the *Boston Herald*—it was something we kept quiet about even within the family. In the era of Senator Joseph McCarthy and his congressional witch-hunts, my parents, a schoolteacher and a businessman, like many others, were really scared.

It was only when I got to Harvard College in 1953 that I began to get a sense of emerging trends that were challenging societal values. The Harvard of the 1950s was still a relatively conservative place. One of its dominant features was the prominence of students from upper-class families. Yet there were many other cultural threads that made Harvard an exciting place to be. I was drawn to those that were counter-cultural. I spent time in circles of people who were rebelling against the conservative social attitudes of the 1950s. I was attracted to subcultures that were marginalized by those attitudes or that were overtly defying societal norms. While contrarian, these movements were not political—they did not involve struggles for social change. But they were raising questions about the values of society in ways that were to lead to the movements of the 1960s.

A group of us who were fans of be-bop and cool jazz went regularly to Boston clubs where blacks and whites mixed, clubs such as Storyville and the Hi-Hat. The music didn't have the political content of the 1960s—there was no Joan Baez or Arlo Guthrie—but its social setting was counter-cultural. And, there was Billie Holiday's "Strange Fruit," the powerfully moving song about the lynching of blacks in the South. When the be-bop saxophonist Charlie Parker died in 1955, we gathered at a local record producer's apartment for a "wake." A classmate who was one of our group, Jack Correa, knew a lot of jazz musicians and read poetry to jazz music. Jack threw an absinthe party where we drank his homemade concoction and imagined ourselves as budding Rimbauds or Baudelaires.

The Beat movement of poets and writers was more openly rebellious. I had read On the Road and other books by Jack Kerouac and fancied myself as part of that movement. On one occasion, a group of scruffy men appeared to attend a poetry reading at my undergraduate dormitory, Adams House. (Harvard students were still required to wear jacket and tie in those days.) I learned that one of them was Gregory Corso, my favorite Beat poet. He and his friends had moved in across the street and began to appear at events in Adams House. When Allen Ginsberg, Peter Orlovsky, and Corso came to Harvard's Lowell Lecture Hall, my friends and I listened to them recite their poetry—defiant, profane, sexual, homosexual—often to the rhythm of be-bop. The performers were lubricated onstage with a jug of red wine. Starting to identify myself with this world, I began to wear a black glove on one hand.

Through my connections on the literary scene, I met many gay students. Homosexuality was much more acceptable in literary and artistic circles than in other sectors of society. In these environments within Harvard, gays felt more comfortable being open about their homosexuality. I found their company intellectually stimulating; I made many friends. From them, I heard stories of persecution. Some of them had been called before one of the Harvard deans who admonished them for their homosexual behavior. One friend was rushed out of Cambridge by Harvard because of his affair with a townie—the term used to describe non-Harvard Cambridge residents. I had so many gay friends that one of them—convinced I was really gay—told Barbara that she was a good "cover" for me.

In many ways I was an observer, not a participant, in each of these subcultures. I was not gay, I was not a Beat poet, and my jazz piano playing was rudimentary. Some of the people I mixed with were outsiders in society by their own choice and some because of societal attitudes. But I saw values in these subcultures that I felt much closer to than those of the mainstream at Harvard. These outsider values were even responsible for my meeting Barbara, my wife-to-be. At a student party in Eliot House, we found common ground in our interest in Colin Wilson's recently published book, The Outsider.

The closest I got to any overtly political influences was at a dinner held by my left-wing uncle and aunt. He had invited two other students, Michael Tanzer from Harvard and Deborah Wolf from Radcliffe. At one point, my uncle turned to me and asked, "What would you think if I told you that South Korea invaded North Korea?" I was floored by the question and even more so by the support my uncle got from the two students. Almost thirty years later, I met Michael Tanzer again, and discovered that he and several other left-wing students in my class had met regularly for political discussions during our college years. They did so in secret out of fears of McCarthy-like persecution. In 1982, Michael and I were part of a group of classmates organizing a symposium for our twenty-fifth reunion. The group, including those who had met secretly in the 1950s, put together a panel that took a strong stand against the use, maintenance, and testing of nuclear weapons. Some members of this group, like Michael, had long since come out in the open politically. Others, like myself, had progressively arrived at a similar critique of society.

In 1957, I entered graduate school at Harvard, still maintaining many of the same interests and contacts. There were few social and cultural influences in the Chemistry Department other than its conservative atmosphere. The only taste of politics I can remember resulted from my own efforts. Some friends of mine in other labs complained of oppressive working conditions—faculty members who needed to "publish or perish" pushing students to work extreme hours and criticizing them for any outside activities. One student had even been chastised for reading a nonscientific book while he was waiting for an experiment to run its course. The professor said such books would "take his mind off his work." Although I was perfectly happy with the environment in Lowell Hager's lab, the despair of my friends stimulated me to write a letter to the student newspaper, the *Harvard Crimson*. In it I decried what I saw as a stifling apprenticeship imposed on students and the efforts to restrict their intellectual curiosity. I asked for changes that would allow students the opportunity to become "more responsible human beings" as well as excellent chemists.

My concern over the education of scientists was largely stimulated by two then-recent public dramatizations of the problems of science and society. The first was the ongoing saga of J. Robert Oppenheimer, the nuclear physicist who had led the effort to develop the atomic bomb. Oppenheimer later regretted his contributions to the development of nuclear weapons. Because of this "disloyalty" and because of his political associations, he lost his government security clearance and was publicly shamed. Oppenheimer became a symbol of the dilemma of the scientist who chooses to face up to his or her social responsibility. The second event was the widely proclaimed publication in 1959 of C. P. Snow's book *The Two Cultures and the Scientific Revolution*. Snow, with credentials as a research chemist and as a novelist, argued that there was a severe communications breach between scientists on the one hand and those in the humanities on the other. He castigated both sides for their ignorance of each other's fields. Although Snow reserved his sharpest barbs for nonscientists, targeting their lack of scientific knowledge, I latched onto his message about the narrowness of the scientist's training. I connected Snow's questioning of the absence of humanistic training of scientists with the problems that atomic scientists such as Oppenheimer faced. To me, Oppenheimer's regrets at having participated in the making of the bomb indicated that scientists must have a broader education if they are not to be confronted with the same crisis of conscience. The fact that Oppenheimer did become one of the earliest and most outspoken critics of atomic weaponry perhaps is a testimony to his own unusually broad humanistic background.

The *Crimson* decided that it wanted to do a feature story on the subject and I proceeded to talk to more students and faculty. I was surprised to find they were afraid. Students asked that I not use their stories for fear of retribution. And even one of the older faculty members, the inorganic chemist J. J. Lingane, worried that he would lose his Office of Naval Research Grant if he was quoted. A residue of McCarthyism lived on. I ended up depressed by the effort and dropped the whole idea. Decades later, in 1998, the suicides of graduate students in the Chemistry Department at Harvard prompted soul-searching about the conditions of work in that department. The published accounts sounded little different from the events I observed in the late 1950s.

I was to leave the Chemistry Department sooner than I had expected. Lowell had been denied tenure at Harvard and was moving to the University of Illinois at Urbana-Champaign. Bob Williams and I would follow him to finish our thesis work there. I have always connected the failure of Harvard to promote Lowell with that Ping-Pong ball bouncing off the office door on the day of our first meeting. I felt that the very qualities that attracted me to his lab and made it a comfortable place to work were qualities that went against the Harvard grain.

I spent only a few months in Illinois completing my Ph.D. and then moved on to Berkeley in December of 1960. My first day on the campus, I was surprised by the array of soap-box orators stationed near Sproul Plaza. One of them, the sociologist Maurice Zeitlin, had just returned from Cuba. He decried the increasingly hostile attitude of the Eisenhower administration to that country and described what he saw as the socially progressive programs that Fidel Castro was implementing for the Cuban people. Although I, like many others, had initially been enchanted by Castro's victory in 1958, the propaganda of the U.S. government had raised questions in my mind about where that country was headed. I challenged Maury on the sources of his knowledge and was overwhelmed with the depth of his experience in and knowledge of Cuba. This radical and public attack on the U.S. government was something I had never been exposed to in Cambridge. I was still a liberal at heart, but seeds were being sown for future changes.

My exposure to a politically active environment largely ended when Barbara and I moved to Princeton. The quietude there was punctuated only by the presence of Maury Zeitlin, who had moved to Princeton. I had not seen Maury in Berkeley since that first encounter and now he was living practically next door to us. Curious, I learned more about Cuba from Maury. Joining these discussions was the philosopher Robert Nozick, then a socialist but later a libertarian. Bob would apply his logical philosophical training to these discussions. His Socratic questioning forced us to explore our own thinking more deeply. When, in 1962, the Cuban missile crisis arose, my wife and I joined a small group including Maury, Bob, and their wives, Marilyn and Barbara, in a march around the Princeton town square. Afraid and angry, we were critical of the bellicose attitude coming out of Washington. Barbara and I marched with a stroller—Benjamin had been born in Princeton in December 1961. This was our first protest demonstration.

In 1963, we moved to London, and looked for a way to continue our political activity. We joined a massive international march in London to protest against nuclear weapons. One of the leaders of the march was Gregory Lambrakis, a prominent left-wing figure in Greece. Later that year, Barbara and I were sitting at a café in Patras, Greece, when we noticed two men at the next table crying as they read the newspaper. We saw a picture of Lambrakis on the front page and asked what had happened. He had been assassinated by right-wing thugs hired by Greek military officers. This assassination and the resulting trials of military officers were portrayed in the now-classic 1969 Costa-Gavras film Z. We heard many say that the United States bore some responsibility for what had happened in Greece. Just a few months after Lambrakis was killed, John F. Kennedy was assassinated in the United States.

During my last year in Europe, when I was working at the Institut Pasteur in Paris, I became even more committed to political activity. Political discussion was the norm in the lab; French culture was much more ideologically polarized than that of the United States. Most of the scientists and students were left-wingers. Jacob's student François Cuzin, who worked in the next lab, was a member of the Communist Party and constantly engaged me in arguments over U.S. foreign policy. He challenged the U.S government's rationalization for its 1965 invasion of the Dominican Republic. I defended "my country," but enough had happened over the years to weaken my remaining defenses. I could no longer support the international politics of the United States. A few months later, a group of American postdocs from the Institut Pasteur, including Ethan Signer and me, went to the U.S. Embassy to protest the escalating involvement in Vietnam.

Just as important, during this year in Paris, I discovered the American expatriate scene. My introduction to it came about through a visit from my absinthe-making college friend Jack Correa and his wife, Peggy. Jack had opened a nightclub in Florence, Italy, called The Red Garter, a hot spot for U.S. soldiers stationed in Europe. One of these GIs was a San Franciscan, James Orem, who, after finishing his tour of duty in Greece, stopped by Florence and became good friends with Jack. Jim then moved to Paris, prompting Jack's visit. We all got together for dinner one night and Jim and I immediately hit it off. Jim was a writer, working for a small English-language newspaper in Paris, the *Paris Gazette*. We shared a love of books and began exchanging them—a practice that ended only with his death in 1998. Jim also introduced me to another life-long habit, drinking Calvados.

Jim Orem and I started to hang out together at Left Bank places where American expatriates gathered. These included the Café de Seine on rue de Seine and Buttercup's Chicken Shack in Montparnasse, a jazz club run by the wife of the jazz musician Bud Powell. Sometimes we would end up late at night in Buttercup's room in the Hotel La Louisiane, also on rue de Seine. There, I met mostly black Americans who were at least temporarily expatriates because of racism in the United States. Now, not only was I getting a dose of the French perspective on the foreign policy of my country, but through my acquaintances with African Americans I was getting a deeper understanding of what it means to be black in the United States.

Frank van Brakle, a black journalist who worked at the same newspaper as Jim, had just interviewed the writer James Baldwin: "Paris is a long way from Harlem . . . I can function here. I can't in America. There's too much time lost in being mad, no time for anything else, just anger, hate, and fear." Jim introduced me to Lee Bridges, who wrote poetry and still does in Amsterdam. At Buttercup's I met Curtiss Powell, a biochemist who had completed his Ph.D. in Sweden and was working in a lab in Paris. Frank and Lee were among the older members of the black expatriate community; they had given up all hope for changes in racial attitudes in America and had settled permanently in Europe. Curtiss and other younger blacks were planning to return to the United States and join the struggle led by people such as Malcolm X and Martin Luther King. They were not resigned like the older expatriates; they were angry. And they got even angrier when the French government, acting at the request of the United States, refused to allow Malcolm X entry into France after he arrived at Orly Airport. His visit had been eagerly awaited by Curtiss and many other blacks, and I was almost as frustrated and upset as they were when it was not allowed. I was to meet Curtiss again in 1970 after his release from a New York prison, where he had been incarcerated for his activities as a Black Panther (see Chapter 4).

Over the years, accumulating experiences had changed my political sensitivities—my understanding of racism, which grew from involvement in the jazz scene in the 1950s and experiences with black expatriates in Paris; my views of U.S. foreign policy, which were informed by events in Cuba, the Dominican Republic, Greece, and most prominently Vietnam; my views of the stifling or oppressive aspects of American culture, which developed from exposure to the rebellion of the Beats and the anguish of gays in the conservative 1950s. But one of the problems I was still not sensitive to was the treatment of women. I blithely went out drinking and talking with Jim and his friends, sometimes several nights a week, leaving Barbara at home in Vanves, a suburb of Paris, to take care of our two boys (Anthony was born in Cambridge, England, in 1964).

When we returned to Boston in 1965, I was ready to get more

seriously involved in political activities. It didn't take long. There were protest demonstrations against the Vietnam War to join and help organize. Mahlon Hoagland, a professor in my department, had taken the responsibility of collecting Harvard Medical School faculty signatures on antiwar petitions and ads to be placed in the *New York Times*. He asked if I would be willing to take over this responsibility. I became a member of the organizing committee of BAFGOPI, the Boston Area Faculty Group on Public Issues, which circulated the petitions. At BAFGOPI meetings, I met local leftist professors such as the geneticist Salvador Luria, the linguist Noam Chomsky, the paleontologist Stephen Jay Gould, the historian Howard Zinn, and the philosopher of science Hilary Putnam.

As I collected signatures at the Medical School, I came to find out which faculty members took a critical look at prevailing governmental and institutional policies and were willing to be outspoken on these issues. This information became important to me in 1968, when Martin Luther King was assassinated. No event has influenced me more than King's death. Like many others, I felt the loss of hope. But, also like many others, I have an optimistic streak. My immediate reaction was to call up Edward Kravitz, one of the Medical School faculty members who I knew would be feeling the same way I did. "We have to do something at the Med School, Ed." We contacted other sympathetic professors. A group of seven of us began to meet. Our purpose: to find ways in which Harvard Medical School could institute changes that would open up opportunities for African Americans

Luigi Gorini, an older professor whose lab was right next to mine, was part of the group. Like the Frenchmen François Jacob and Jacques Monod, Luigi, an Italian, had been politically engaged by World War II and the events that preceded it. Luigi was one of the few scientists who refused to sign Mussolini's Fascist oath in the 1930s. He was forced to leave his university position; he then joined the Italian resistance movement and worked in a succession of small pharmaceutical houses. One of his duties in the resistance was raising money to support the struggle against Fascism. He would threaten bankers with dire consequences if they didn't give some specified amount to the resistance movement. Toward the end of the war, he and his wife-to-be, Annamaria Torriani, established a rehabilitation center in northern Italy for Jewish children just liberated from concentration camps. As a result of their refugee work, Luigi and Annamaria's names are enshrined in Yad Vashem, the monument in Israel that, among other things, honors those gentiles who showed courage in helping Jews during the Holocaust. (Varian Fry, the friend of my uncle and of François Williams's father, has also been honored at Yad Vashem, the only American so honored.) Luigi and Annamaria's idealism and political activism had not diminished upon their move to the United States.

Luigi's passion, his unflagging outrage at injustice, was to be a constant inspiration to me until he died in 1976. I would often run into him in the hallway of our floor, brandishing the latest issue of the New York Times and yelling about the latest crime committed by the U.S. government. I might not always have agreed with him, but seeing a man in his seventies who could hold so strongly to his ideals strengthened my own resolve.

Our group developed proposals and went to the Medical School dean, Robert Ebert, to convince him that changes in policies toward minorities were necessary. We discovered that out of 150 medical students in each year's class, the average number of African Americans was 0.5. We argued that the Medical School should set aside funds to support minority students with the goal of admitting 15 African American students every year. We also proposed changes in programs and policies for the hiring and training of minorities, largely to help the neighboring black community of

Roxbury. The dean agreed to support our proposals and called a faculty meeting to consider the call for increased admission of minority students. Our major success was the implementation of the recommendation for minority admissions to the Medical School. The group chose me to make the presentation of this recommendation to a faculty meeting. Ironically, at this meeting, it was not our historical, moral, or political arguments that seemed to carry the day with the faculty. Rather, I persuaded them that times were changing, that African Americans would be some of the leaders in U.S. medicine in the future, and that if Harvard wanted to continue to be in the position of training the leaders, it had better get in at the beginning. We had played down our strong political feelings to achieve our goal.

A year later, in April 1969, the growing politicization of American society hit Harvard in dramatic fashion. A group of students with a list of demands occupied University Hall, the administrative headquarters of Harvard. Although Harvard made some moves to respond to these demands, Nathan Pusey, the president, eventually approved the removal of the students by police. The brutality of the police action—they wielded batons and bloodied heads—brought national attention to the campus. It brought to my attention one of the occupying students' demands that surprised me and goaded me into action. Harvard had been buying up residential property in the Mission Hill section of Roxbury, which abuts Harvard Medical School. There were plans to build a new hospital and faculty housing on the property; architectural drawings had already been prepared. To speed things up, the real estate agencies, which were acting as fronts for Harvard, had been using slum landlord techniques to force tenants out of the buildings Harvard had bought. The buildings were allowed to deteriorate and when people did move out, the houses either were boarded up or were rented to rowdy groups such as motorcycle gangs. The community being uprooted was racially mixed and working class, made up largely of families. For them, it had become an unpleasant place to live.

The students that occupied University Hall demanded that Harvard restore the community and drop its development plans. The publicity generated by the students' demands forced Harvard to negotiate with the community. Harvard established a committee that included Harvard officials, one of the Harvard students who had drawn up the demands, and Mission Hill tenants of Harvard. Dismayed by what I had learned of the situation, I asked to be made a member of this committee. I wanted to make sure that Harvard dealt fairly with the Mission Hill residents. After months of negotiation it became apparent that the formation of the committee was only a sop to the tenants and plans were moving ahead to destroy the community. I began to organize Medical School faculty, staff, and students to protest these policies. The tenants themselves had already been catalyzed into action by the Harvard students and had formed the Roxbury Tenants of Harvard organization. After I led a protest occupation of Dean Ebert's office, the dean agreed to go with me and Robert Parks, president of the tenants' organization, on a tour of the housing. We showed him the deterioration of the neighborhood and the boarded-up houses. As a result of all the protests, the tenants' perseverance, and the publicity that actions such as this received, Harvard was finally forced to negotiate an acceptable compromise. The hospital would go up in a more limited space; much of the housing would be saved and rehabilitated; and Harvard would help the tenants build and run Mission Park, an attractive housing project in the same neighborhood.

I had worked with a multiracial community of people that had united in struggle and acted together to improve their living conditions. Their example at the community level was as inspiring to me as that of Luigi Gorini was at a personal level. The evolution of this community and, on a larger scale, the successes of the civil rights movement gave me hope that societies could change for the better.

Yet none of my hope and social activism of the late 1960s related to my life as a scientist. This chapter and the preceding one appear to describe two separate lives that happened to occur in the same set of places over the same fifteen-year period: the evolution of a scientist and the evolution of a political activist. I could explain the origins of my political activism simply by listing the social influences I was exposed to over the years. But I may have been receptive to those influences because of a personal need. Even when I had overcome my early misgivings about becoming a scientist, I still wanted a life that included intellectual activity in realms other than science. I found that my political activities satisfied that need. But now, I realized that I also wanted to feel that my life was integrated, that these two realms—the scientific and the political—need not be separate. What brought the life of the scientist and the social activist together was partly this need and partly outside events that occurred in 1969. The connection was made when I called the press conference in November 1969.

By 1969, the turmoil over civil rights and the Vietnam War had seeped into the American scientific community, despite its lack of a political culture. The attacks on governmental policy in other areas led some of us in science to question the directions and uses of government-sponsored science itself. This questioning began with physicists who criticized the use of their basic scientific research to develop weapons used in Vietnam and described as "the electronic battlefield." Activism was more the rule in the physics community, as physicists had borne the burden of guilt for the development of atomic weapons. But 1969 was also the year that the psychologist Arthur Jensen claimed that blacks were genetically inferior to whites in intelligence. The publication of his article in the *Harvard Educational Review* ensured widespread publicity for his arguments that compensatory education programs were doomed to failure. Biologists began to challenge the misrepresentations of genetics in Jensen's article. This unaccustomed questioning of the uses of science by physicists and biologists culminated in the formation of the organization Scientists and Engineers for Social and Political Action (soon renamed Science for the People) and the influential call for a national strike by MIT science students in 1969.

It was in this context that, in the fall of 1969, my colleagues and I decided to use our isolation of a gene as an opportunity to heighten public awareness of the potential social consequences of genetics research. We stated: "As we see it, scientists are obligated to inform the public about what is happening in their secluded fields of research so that people can demand control over decisions which profoundly affect their lives." These kinds of statements were also to profoundly affect my own life.

Becquerel's discovery of radioactivity in 1896 and the use of an atomic weapon against human beings in 1945 . . . If we do not [work for radical political change], we will one day be a group of very regretful Oppenheimers."

Again, Oppenheimer was motivating my activism, as he had my attempt to mobilize students in the Chemistry Department in the 1950s. I had grown up in the forties and fifties—in the shadow of atomic weapons. I had been exposed to the postwar public soul-searching of atomic scientists. It is true that by the time of our press conference in 1969, the dilemma of these physicists had begun to fade as a symbol for issues of social responsibility in science. But it was still important to me, a strong influence on my thinking and behavior. Today, the awareness of the crisis confronting the nuclear physicists of that earlier period is no longer fresh in the minds of scientists. Because science education does not include reference to controversies surrounding the social impact of science, science students lose a part of their history—and, in my view, a part of their humanity.

▲ ▲ ▲ Our suggestion that there might not be "ample time" to deal with the prospect of genetic engineering was derided by other scientists. Yet within five years, the revolution we had predicted was in full swing. The ability of biologists to readily manipulate genes was upon us more quickly than even we had imagined. The technique of "recombinant DNA," first reported in 1973, would revolutionize biology. Our earlier success at cloning and even purifying a gene had immediate applications only for studies in bacteria, but recombinant DNA technology allowed the isolation of genes from any organism. To make gene-sized fragments required only cutting up the DNA of chromosomes using enzymes that would recognize frequently found specific sites on the DNA. The

DNA could then be packaged ("recombined") into small chromosomes such as those of viruses, put back into a living organism, and readily studied in the laboratory.

This rapid progress confounded the predictions that scientists had made in response to our warning. It also led to an unprecedented action by leading biologists. In 1973, a group that included the geneticists Jim Watson and Paul Berg, called for a moratorium on the use of this new technique. They acted in response to challenges by younger scientists who warned of the potential health hazards of recombinant DNA experiments. They worried, for example, that geneticists were creating viruses and bacteria that had never existed before and that might spread new forms of disease. The moratorium took hold while researchers explored the issues that had been raised.

The unexpected breakthroughs that had permitted the ready manipulation of genes made me realize that one should never say never about the prospects for some scientific development. One cannot safely predict whether a particular scientific achievement will be possible, and certainly not even roughly how long it will take to come to fruition. The ability to readily manipulate genes with the recombinant DNA technique appeared suddenly and surprisingly on the scene, and it evolved from an obscure, unexpected corner of basic bacterial genetic research. A small number of scientists had worked for decades on how bacteria are able to recognize when they are being invaded by foreign DNA and how they destroy that DNA. I among others had always considered this project only a sidebar to the mainstream of progress in molecular biology. However, after decades of research, scientists discovered that the ability to destroy foreign DNA was due to the presence in the bacteria of enzymes that could cleave DNA at specific sites, sites that the bacteria had modified on its own DNA so that it would not be touched. With this discovery, they realized that they had in their hands tools (restriction enzymes) for producing small specific pieces of chromosomes—even gene-sized pieces. This hitherto obscure corner of biology generated several Nobel Prizes. I imagine that the moment of insight these scientists had may have been similar to our own in 1969 when we realized that our viruses carrying the lac genes in their DNA would allow us to purify one of those genes. As with the discovery of restriction enzymes, our studies unexpectedly provided new tools for biologists.

▲ ▲ ▲ The consequences of our press conference mushroomed. Previously seen as a rising star in molecular biology, I now had become, to many in science, a traitor—raising doubts in the public's mind about the unalloyed benefits of the scientific enterprise. My laboratory was in turmoil; some coworkers deplored what we had done, others supported it. Jim Shapiro, who had joined me in the press conference, publicly announced when we appeared together on the *Today* show that he could no longer continue doing science in a society that so misused the products of science. In an interview with a Welsh newspaper, the *South Wales Echo*, he explained: "I am dropping out of science because it is simply being exploited by the people who run this country to serve their own ends. To work in a laboratory is futile at the present time. The only useful mode of life I can imagine now is to challenge the present political system." These are almost the same words that François Williams would use thirty years later in telling me why he had quit science at about the same time. Jim was shortly to leave my lab and spend two years teaching science in Cuba.

A *New York Times* reporter, Robert Reinhold, asked if he could spend time in my lab researching an article on how a new molecular biology lab works. Adhering to the collective spirit of the late sixties, our lab group met and after heated discussions decided that I should tell Reinhold we were not interested. Typical of the times, the argument that held sway in our discussions was that the article would probably focus on me and reinforce the "cult of the personality," ignoring the collective nature of science.

The press conference instantaneously made me into a supposedly knowledgeable spokesperson on the social impact of science. I was invited to speak on the dangers of genetic research, to write books, and to talk on the subject on television talk shows, such as the Today show. I was asked to give a presentation at the Harvard Medical School about my concerns. Before a small group of faculty members, I gave my first speech about social responsibility in science. I remember speaking in a mumble, reading from a prepared text, because I was nervous about my lack of background on the subject—aware that this was not a subject I had thought deeply about.

Inevitably, I was put in the position of having to explain my concerns in greater depth than at the press conference. For the first time, I began to think, read, and write about science and society, attempting to flesh out exactly what it was that worried me about my own research field. I joined the organization Science for the People, an activist group that brought together scientists from many different disciplines. We discussed the social influences on the directions science took. We focused on the ways in which science was used to benefit only the wealthier segments of society and operated to the detriment of the less privileged. Science for the People would become the center of my social activism for the next two decades.

This learning experience, this activism, was to play a large role in events that followed shortly after the 1969 press conference. In January 1970, I received a letter telling me that I had been named winner of that year's Eli Lilly Award in Microbiology and Immunology by the American Society of Microbiology. The award, sponsored by Eli Lilly Pharmaceuticals, was given each year to a young microbiologist under the age of thirty-five who had made outstanding scientific contributions to the field. The award consisted of a cash prize of $1,000 and a bronze medal. I was surprised and happy to receive the recognition. But, at the same time, I felt conflicted. In the growing politicized environment of science, and in Science for the People, in particular, there was strong criticism of the misuses of science by both the government and industry. Pharmaceutical companies were considered among the worst industrial "villains," foisting useless or overpriced drugs on the population. How could I accept money from one of them? I discussed my dilemma with some of those in the lab who were most sensitive to the issues. They agreed that it was indeed a dilemma. I felt that I either had to refuse the prize or use it to make a statement by donating the money to a worthy cause. I chose the latter course, in a sense, following the tradition my colleagues and I had started with the press conference.

But to what organization should I give the prize? This decision was made easy for me by events that were set in motion nearly a year earlier. On the morning of April 1, 1969, twenty-one black men and women, members of the Black Panther Party, were rounded up by the New York City police, charged with conspiracy, and sent to jail. Among the charges were plotting to murder New York City policeman, to dynamite the New York Botanical Gardens, and to spread rat urine on the entryways of New York City police stations. This group came to be known as the Panther 21, later the Panther 13 after eight of them were released. I had followed the case of the Panther 21 and the well-publicized police and government confrontations with the Panthers. Late in 1969, two Black Panther leaders, Mark Clark and Fred Hampton, were killed during a police raid in Chicago. Several members of the Black Panther party in Los Angeles were wounded during a gun battle with police. There was enough official and media questioning of these and other police actions to raise suspicions of a government conspiracy to destroy the Panthers. These suspicions were confirmed many years later with the release of government documents under the Freedom of Information Act. While I was dismayed by the persecution of the Panthers, I felt helpless. I didn't see any way in which I could make a difference; my most extreme political activity had been to collect professor's signatures on anti–Vietnam War petitions and to march in antiwar demonstrations.

What eventually connected me much more closely to the plight of the Panthers was a *New York Times* article I read one morning early in 1970. On a back page I came across an article updating the situation of the Panther 21. The article ended with a list of names of the jailed Panthers; I was startled to see that a Curtiss Powell, identified as a biochemist, was among them. It must be the same Curtiss Powell, the biochemist whose angry outbursts I remembered from our get-togethers in Buttercup's room at the Hotel La Louisiane in Paris. I began to look more closely into the charges against the 21 and their treatment.

It was shortly after this discovery that I received word of the Eli Lilly Award. It all came together: my dilemma over the prize, over the government persecution of the Black Panthers and of my friend Curtiss Powell. In addition, I came to know more of the Black Panthers' work in the community through a Harvard medical student friend, Michael Williams. Mike was helping out with the Black Panther health and nutrition programs in the black community of nearby Roxbury. I decided that I would give the prize money to the Black Panthers.

The award was announced at the annual meeting of the American Society for Microbiology, held in Boston in late April 1970. At the ceremonies, where several awards were presented, I was handed a check for $1,000 and the medal. Nervous about what I was about to do, I abruptly and awkwardly asked if I could say a few words. I took the microphone and blurted out that I would split the prize money between the Panther Free Health Clinic in Boston and the defense fund for the Panther 13 in New York City. There were gasps, groans, and a smattering of applause. People were too startled to digest what had happened and to react. The ASM officials on the stage simply went on to the next prize, which was for Outstanding Microbiology Teacher of the Year.

The next night I was scheduled to give an hour-long speech as part of the award process. In that speech I reviewed my lab's scientific accomplishments, the work for which I had received the award. But then, half-way through, I left the world of basic science and segued into a discussion of the world where science and society meet:

> It is probably clear from the work I have described that we derive a great deal of pleasure from the type of work we do. The manipulations of genes, practically at will, has been a lot of fun. It is a constant temptation for me to spend all my waking hours thinking and working in this area. However, I believe that this is a temptation that I and other scientists must avoid, for we have a special responsibility in this society because of the way we and our work are used.

I explained my decision to give the prize money to the Black Panther clinic and defense fund. For the rest of the talk, I discussed the social responsibility of scientists. I spoke of how basic science as well as applied science can be used to destructive ends—from the development of atomic weapons to biological warfare research to the use of high-technology weapons in Vietnam. Because of the source of the award—Eli Lilly and Company—I concentrated on the practices of the pharmaceutical industry and talked of the overuse of antibiotics. I pointed to the inflated prices of drugs made possible by the manipulations of drug companies to ensure extending patent rights to their products. I ended by attacking the overwhelming public relations efforts of drug companies—"presents for medical students, lavish dinners for interns, presents for and constant pressure on doctors." These efforts helped guarantee the use, overuse, and sometimes misuse of expensive drug company products.

I no longer mumbled in my speech as I had at Harvard when I first spoke of science and society. In a few short months, I had developed the confidence to explain my views in public. It had been a rapid education.

Outrage and acclaim followed my actions. Officials of the ASM were dismayed. One yelled out in anguish from the audience, "What have you done with our prize?" My actions were reported in the *New York Times* and other newspapers. In the days after these articles appeared, I received anonymous threatening letters: "I hope you are shot by one of these guns" or "It will be pleasant to listen to the death gurgle in your throat after one of your beloved black panthers has slashed it . . . decent people will live to celebrate your death."

These threats were more than balanced by other responses. After the talk, a black researcher from Lilly came up to me and whispered, "Right on, brother!" I received letters from individuals commending my stance, and one group of younger scientists from the University of Wisconsin and another from the New York Public Health Research Institute in New York City each cosigned letters congratulating me on my action. But most important to me were several letters I received from Curtiss Powell himself. Curtiss had read a newspaper account of my ASM speech and my donation and was heartened by my action. He hadn't remembered me, not connecting the Harvard professor cited in the papers with the white guy hanging out in the Café de Seine. He thanked me and lamented that it was "difficult to get scientists to speak out against the repression that is upon us." I answered, reminding him of Paris days, sending him a picture of him and Buttercup that I had cut out of an old *Ebony* magazine.

Curtiss and I stayed in touch. In early 1971, a judge dismissed all the charges against the remaining thirteen Panthers. Curtiss, along with the others, was released after nearly two years in jail. Thomas Benjamin, a virologist at the New York Public Health Research Institute, offered Curtiss a research position. Tom was one of the scientists from the Institute who had signed the letter congratulating me on my Eli Lilly Award speech. We invited Curtiss up from New York to speak to a Science for the People meeting. He would spend several years doing research in Tom Benjamin's lab in New York and then move to Zambia. There, he worked for many years trying to develop a vaccine that would make people resistant to the parasite that causes sleeping sickness.

▲ ▲ ▲ There was little time to catch my breath after the Eli Lilly Award. One week after my speech at the ASM, on May 4, 1970, Kent State University students who had for days been protesting President Nixon's decision to invade Cambodia were shot at by the Ohio National Guard. Four students died of gunshot wounds from the guardsmen's rifles. Only months before the government had come for the Black Panthers. Few spoke out at that time. Now it was the children of white families who were being killed. Outraged students and faculty at campuses across the country declared a strike. A group of us at the Harvard Medical School—students, faculty, and employees—formed a strike steering committee.

Classes at the Harvard Medical School were halted. We organized demonstrations and teach-ins. Many in the group focused on opposition to the war in Vietnam, but I put my efforts into education about the attacks on the Black Panthers. We put together a pamphlet describing the events over the previous year in which so many members of the Panthers had been killed, wounded, or imprisoned. We pointed out the evidence that was available even then, showing that these events were inspired by the government. It may be hard to understand today, but these activities were included in an article in the *Medical School Alumni Bulletin*. The picture of me behind a table offering pamphlets to two respectably dressed faculty members is captioned "Professor Beckwith explains Panther literature." All responses were not respectful, however. One faculty member accused us of "polluting the antiwar movement" with our defense of the Panthers. We responded that he and people who agreed with him were polluting that movement with their racism.

▲ ▲ ▲ I am a shy person. Perhaps I felt emboldened to take these risks to my scientific career because I still felt that my presence and success in science were the result of flukes: the fluke of Bob Williams recommending that I talk with Lowell Hager; the fluke of the move to quiet Princeton, rescuing me from the earthly pleasures and political activism of Berkeley; the fluke of my scientific results attracting attention shortly before I was to become jobless. Remember, in London, I was six months away from the end of my fellowship, of my job, and of my career as a scientist. At each of these junctures, I was on the verge of leaving science. Despite my inspiration with the science of the Institut Pasteur group in the late 1950s, I still had not come to imagine myself as a successful scientist. During the low point in London, with no job in sight for the next year, my thoughts returned to alternative lives as a writer, a historian, or a literary critic. Barbara offered to support me if I chose a new career. Even after I was well established in science at Harvard, I still had the feeling of being a visitor in the world of science, only there by chance. I felt unbelievably lucky to be where I was. For these reasons, no possible negative impact on my scientific career of my political actions appeared as drastic as what might have happened to me without these flukes.

But there were consequences of my activism. I learned of instances where my name had been vetoed as an invited scientific speaker because of my political stands. I was not to receive a significant honor or award for another fourteen years. This lack of prizes could well have been mostly due to the quality of my scientific achievements during that period, but in one case it was clearly due to my actions at the press conference and at the ASM award ceremonies. In 1984, Salvador Luria, a member of the National Academy of Sciences, called me from Washington. He explained that the Genetics Section of the Academy had been considering my election to the Academy for several years. But some members of that section worried that I would reject membership in the Academy or attack it. For those reasons, they did not want to add my name to the list of candidates. After several years of debating this issue, Luria, who was sympathetic to my activities, wanted to be able to tell the group that I would accept. He asked me point-blank what I would do. I told him that it was not an appropriate question—that any decision should be made on the merits. I was finally elected that year.

Many other scientists were taking chances during this period. The scientific community had become much more politically aware and active as a result of the events of the previous few years—the growing antiwar movement, the increasing racial strife, including the attack on the Panthers, the MIT student strike, the founding of Science for the People, our press conference, and my Eli Lilly Award. The activists in science initially came mainly from physics and molecular biology. For the physicists, it was the history of nuclear physics that provided the sensitivity to the social impact of science. The origins of molecular biology as both a scientific and cultural revolution attracted a number of young scientists who were more iconoclastic and questioning than scientists in many other fields, such as the older field of chemistry. Academic chemistry, of course, had also been largely incorporated into the industrial sphere.

Biologists of this generation were among the first U.S. citizens to travel to North Vietnam. In 1970, Mark Ptashne, a molecular biologist at Harvard, was the first American scientist to go to North Vietnam. In 1971, Ethan Signer, my former collaborator, along with Arthur Galston, a biologist from Yale University, visited scientific institutes in China and North Vietnam. These trips were meant to symbolize the opposition of the scientists to the war in Vietnam. The microbiologists David Baltimore and Richard Novick of the New York Public Health Research Institute led the battle to convince the ASM to take a stand against the development of biological weapons. The geneticist Matthew Meselson at Harvard devoted enormous energy to documenting the dangers of biological weapons. With students at Stanford University, the biologist Donald Kennedy, now editor of *Science* magazine, prepared a booklet describing the ecological damage that had been done to the entire country of Vietnam by the spraying of plant killers and by the craters formed by the huge number of bombs dropped.

▲ ▲ ▲ People still ask me after all these years about my decision to donate to the Black Panthers. Many, including me, have now read accounts of the sometimes violent internecine struggles in the organization. They assumed that with all these exposés I would now feel differently. They imagined I would regret an action that had occurred in the heat of the radical moment. It is probably hard for many who did not live through that period to understand fully the degree of governmental repression of the Panthers. Even though the group certainly had its faults, many of its programs were aimed at empowering black people. But, more important, the ability of the government to use illegal and violent means to effectively eliminate a group had to be challenged. It wasn't just that the attack on the Panthers was wrong. A government apparatus established to carry out such subversion could well have moved on to other less radical targets. If uncontested by the public, the government's actions might have been the harbinger of a far more repressive society.

The Tarantella of the Living

Late in 1969, even before our press conference, I began to make plans for a break from the political intensity of the previous two years. The Guggenheim Foundation awarded me a fellowship to do research for six months, starting in the fall of 1970, at an institute in Naples, Italy. I chose the Istituto Internazionale di Genetica e Biofisica (IIGB) because a friend, Glauco Tocchini-Valentini, worked there. Glauco had recently discovered the central role of the enzyme RNA polymerase in the first step in gene expression—the copying of DNA into RNA. This, then, was the enzyme that recognized promoter sites on the DNA and initiated the transcription of RNA. We had begun a collaboration. In Glauco's lab, I would try to prepare more of our purified lac gene and study its expression in the test tube using his preparations of RNA polymerase.

But I also chose Naples as the site for my leave because of my strong impressions of the relaxed atmosphere and the vibrancy of the people at the IIGB. One incident, which took place many years later, has come to symbolize this atmosphere for me.

It is 1988. I have been appointed a member of the Scientific Advisory Board to IIGB. At a meeting of the board, we sit in the director's office evaluating the research programs of the institute's scientists. As we deliberate, humid spring breezes, bearing the scent of tropical plants, wash over us. I notice that an occasional blossom drifts through the open window and floats languidly to the floor. Puzzled, I then see that sometimes a whole plant arcs into our meeting room. Nobody remarks on these mysterious bouquets. At a coffee break, I ask for an explanation. One of the researchers, it seems, lives with her elderly mother and can't bear to leave her at home alone. She brings her mother to the institute and leaves her to fend for herself during the day. The mother roams the grounds of the institute, weeding the gardens. Either because she has mistaken a flower for a weed or perhaps to brighten the day of the hard-working scientists inside, we are the beneficiaries of her floral gift.

The floating flowers punctuating our scientific discussions were emblematic of the culture of this institute. The personal lives of individuals and the problems and tumult of the outside world have always been integrated into its daily scientific life. One can trace this unusual environment back to the founding of the institute.

IIGB had been established in 1962 to introduce into Italy a scientific culture analogous to that in the United States. In Italy, as in most European countries, a tradition of hierarchical structure dominated universities and research institutes. Older professors ruled the roost; younger scientists had to follow the research programs of their professors and rarely were able to develop their own scientific ideas. Assistant professors might rise to the position of professor only when their own professor died or when the death of a professor at another university created a vacancy. Such features of the European system were not widespread in the United States. Young American scientists were increasingly assuming independent assistant professor positions directly after their postdoctoral work. They were no longer simply "assistants" to the senior professor; they could follow their own research programs. The independence of young scientists was even more pronounced in molecular biology than in other scientific disciplines. Because of the dramatic successes in this field and the cultural revolution that accompanied it, a new crop of brash young scientists appeared on the international scene. The success of younger scientists such as Jim Watson paved the way for the independence of the new generation.

The scientific successes of the American system inspired the influential Italian biologist Adriano Buzzatti-Traverso to try to establish a similar environment in Italy. He pushed for the creation of a scientific institute that would operate according to the American system. It would present, Buzzatti hoped, an example that would stimulate change in Italy. Italian officials were persuaded by Buzzatti. Further, they saw this proposal as a way to support another ongoing governmental program, "cassa per il mezzogiorno"— cash for the economically underdeveloped South. Along with certain industries that were being moved to southern Italy, the establishment of a scientific institute in Naples, it was hoped, would help boost the economy of the region. Thus, from its inception, the institute brought with it a host of scientific, cultural, and political aspirations.

In 1962, with Buzzatti's plan approved, the laboratories of IIGB were set up in "temporary barracks" in the Fuorigrotta district of Naples. Fuorigrotta (outside the tunnel) is the northern district of Naples, which is connected to the center of the city by a tunnel dug through a steep hill. The low-rise buildings of IIGB contrast with the adjacent massive Naples soccer stadium and the exhibition park Mostra D'Oltremare (built by Mussolini) down the road. The human scale of the institute's buildings resonates with its culture. Even though the facilities have become quite dilapidated over the decades, as of the year 2000, the institute was still housed in the "temporary barracks." Despite the limitations imposed by the aging laboratories, IIGB has trained a sizable fraction of the molecular biologists now working in Italy. The productivity of the IIGB scientists under these conditions is a testimony to their resourcefulness and to their good humor.

At the institute's inception, Buzzatti recruited several prominent older scientists to fill some of IIGB's "barracks." Many of these scientists, who agreed with Buzzatti's vision, came from the more economically advanced northern parts of Italy. During these early years, the institute also recruited younger scientists, fresh from their postdoctoral experience, to start their own labs. These included researchers such as Glauco, who had just finished training at the University of Geneva and with Sydney Brenner in Cambridge; Pablo Amati, who had worked with Matt Meselson at Harvard; and Maurizio Iaccarino, who had studied protein synthesis with Paul Berg at Stanford.

I first visited IIGB in 1964 to give an invited talk on my research. The young scientists I met were as enthusiastic and as serious about their work as scientists anywhere. Still, they appeared to take a more humorous and less intense attitude toward life than the people I had been working with in more northern climes. Something—the weather, the immediate environment, the Neapolitan culture—seemed to infect people with lightness and charm. That trip still stands out in my mind as a welcoming, warm experience. Many years later, I came across a passage in Harold Acton's *The Bourbons of Naples* that matched my impressions of life at IIGB and in Naples in general:

> There is nothing of the bee-hive or ant-heap here, and pray heaven there never will be. Humanity predominates. To those who are dulled by routine, by modern mechanizations, fog, smog, cold murky climates and the fatigue du Nord, Naples offers an invitation to join the tarantella of the living while there is time.

On this visit, I hit it off particularly with Rita Arditti, an Argentinian postdoctoral fellow who was doing genetic research with Enrico Calef. Calef had made some of the most important contributions to understanding how the DNA of bacterial viruses such as ϕ80 and λ (viruses we had used in our purification of the lac gene DNA) becomes part of *Escherichia coli*'s chromosome. Rita came to Boston the following year, 1965, to work as a postdoctoral fellow in biochemistry at Brandeis University. We—Barbara and I and our two sons, Ben and Anthony—became close friends with Rita, her son, Federico, and Paolo Strigini, who lived with Rita and was a postdoctoral fellow with Luigi Gorini. Through Rita, we came to know other Italians in the Boston area who had come from IIGB—Franco and Annamaria Guerrini, Lia Fischer-Fantuzzi, and Cesare Vesco. We met Glauco when he came to Boston and visited with our friends. Along with John Scaife and a graduate student from MIT, Richard D'Ari, Barbara and I did much of our socializing with this group of Italians. In 1967, Rita came to me to say that she would like to switch labs and do some genetics again. Would I have space and money for her? I did.

Rita was very active politically, first in the politics of science and later in the women's liberation movement. She was one of the first people in Boston to join the fledgling Science for the People chapter. Our political conversations and her prodding played a large role in stimulating my own activism in science, beginning in late 1969. Later, Rita was to leave laboratory research and take a professorship with Union Institute, a floating graduate program formed by a consortium of small colleges. She has remained active politically as one of the founders of New Words, the first women's book store in the Boston area, and as the author of several books, including the recent *Searching for Life*, about the grandmothers of the Plaza de Mayo of Argentina.

The Italians we knew in Boston reminded me, with their openness and sense of humor, of my visit to IIGB. They were deeply involved in their scientific work, had a broad cultural background, and shared a political, but also ironic perspective on human activities. My attraction to the milieu they created contributed to my choice of IIGB as a place to spend my leave. It would also offer a chance to recharge my scientific batteries.

Events at IIGB in the spring of 1970—after my decision to go there—made my choice of venue for a stay in Naples even more interesting to me. The establishment of this research institute that did not follow the traditional hierarchical pattern of Italian science had opened the floodgates for even more revolutionary views of science. The political environment within science in the late 1960s and early 1970s became increasingly radical on both sides of the Atlantic. Because of its own cultural roots, molecular biology was often the hub of such political activism. In the Netherlands, "science shops"—small neighborhood centers where scientists interacted with and helped the public—were established. In France, after the uprisings of May 1968, scientists and staff at the Institut Pasteur and other institutes met in assemblies to debate institute policies. The most radical of these activities by scientists took place at IIGB. Early in 1970, a group of researchers and other institute workers presented a list of demands to the institute leadership. Dissatisfied with the response, they staged an occupation of the labs that was to last for several months. All research stopped.

The occupiers demanded democratization of the institute: equalization of pay for all workers, participatory decision making on the scientific directions of research programs, and education of institute workers to raise their ability to contribute to laboratory research. Those occupying the institute came from all levels of employees, from researchers to support staff. After a six-month siege and stand-off, the protesters agreed to reopen the institute; in exchange they were granted one of the barracks in which they could implement their plans for democratization. The rest of the institute returned more or less to pre-occupation conditions. The occupation resulted in enormous divisions and enmity between people within the institute. I saw the occupation, for better or worse, as yet another indication of the lack of borders between IIGB and the outside world.

My family and I arrived in Naples in September 1970. Enrico Calef, who was now shuttling between Rome and Naples, sublet his apartment to us. On a hillside in the Posillipo region of Naples, it overlooked the city, the medieval Castel dell Ovo jutting out into the bay of Naples, Mount Vesuvius, and the island of Capri. Our sons attended the John F. Kennedy School of Naples, located in the Mostra d'Oltremare, near the institute. One of the teachers at the school was Dick D'Ari, our Boston friend, who had dropped out of science and moved to Naples. Like ourselves, he had been attracted to Naples because of the friendships he had developed in Boston with Neapolitans.

My arrival in Naples took place shortly after the end of the occupation. Intense discussions and arguments, often approaching physical confrontation, were frequent occurrences outside my lab window. A number of researchers whose work had been interrupted and who were upset by the occupation began to leave. Not only were they dismayed by what had happened, but they also had never been enthusiastic about the culture of Naples since most were not native Neapolitans. By contrast, some of the institute workers who were nonscientific staff began to take courses in science and started to do laboratory work. To this day, decision making on the Scientific Advisory Board involves staff from all positions—office worker, stockroom employee, and researcher. This was true for the whole institute, not just the portion inhabited by the former occupiers.

Glauco asked his technician, Bruno Esposito, to assist me in my research. Bruno did not speak English, and so I was forced to expand my limited Italian. As I talked with Bruno, I discovered that his position in the lab was a direct consequence of the occupation.

His first job at the institute had been in the carpentry shop, where his father worked. With the democratizing influence of the occupation, Bruno was encouraged to take science courses. His education would be supported by the institute. As a result, Bruno had risen in status from carpenter to research assistant. Ironically, he regretted leaving his former position, where he could walk out of the institute at any time and take a passegiata (stroll) under "il sole."

Naples is not a rich city; it is one of the poorest in Italy. Much of the center of the city is a dark warren of streets, many of its inhabitants living in small, cramped quarters. Yet the Neapolitans are a spirited people—their enthusiasm inspired perhaps by the limpid air and the beauty of the city's surroundings. This was the spirit I had sensed upon my first visit to Naples. The energy of the scientists at IIGB showed that this zest for life did not interfere with a productive scientific career (except for the occupation). And Bruno, despite his misgivings at the time, still works as a research assistant; his name appears on scientific papers from the institute.

There were many signs of the engagement of IIGB scientists with the world beyond the walls of the institute. I discussed with Franco Guerrini his contribution to a book edited by the Italian Communist politician Enrico Berlinguer. Franco's chapter would reflect a Communist view of science and its role in society. He proposed that humans were born with a "senso di proprieta" (a sense or need for property), the basis of capitalist inclinations. This human genetic propensity made achieving the socialist state very difficult. For socialism to succeed, geneticists must find the gene for this "senso" and devise a way to counteract or excise it. A number of researchers from the "democratized" section of the institute had established scientific links with Cuba and were teaching molecular biology courses to Cuban students. Some were changing their research interests to respond to the needs of third world peoples.

Glauco assigned a medical student from the University of Naples, Paolo Bazzicalupo, to work with me on a genetic project. Paolo asked one day if I would meet with a group of science students from the university to tell them what was happening in the politics of science in the United States. My attempt to escape the political intensity of the U.S. had been only partly successful.

The tradition of cultural and political engagement that marks the history of IIGB continues to this day. Paolo, now leading a research team at the institute, is part of a group of scientists who have co-organized with the Istituto Italiano per gli Studi Filosofici (Italian Institute for the Study of Philosophy) of Naples a series of symposia and talks on the interface of science and society.

Both within and outside the laboratory, I quickly learned about Neapolitan culture. One of my first errands in Naples was to open a checking account. Sometime during my first week in the lab, I put on my jacket and started to walk out the door to go to the nearest bank. Glauco stopped me.

"Where are you going?"

"To open up a bank account."

"You can't do that on your own. You have to have a friend at the bank. Hold on a minute. I'll get my secretary. She knows one of the tellers at the bank down the street."

("Why do I need a friend at the bank for me to give them my money," I wondered.)

So, I walked with Glauco's secretary to the bank, where she signaled to one of the tellers. He came over to us furtively, as though performing a forbidden act, and after a rapid exchange in the local dialect, the teller agreed that I would be allowed to open a checking account.

This trip to the bank was only the first of many such negotiations I experienced or observed. The base of Neapolitan culture and its economy is the exchange of favors—favors that, to the outsider at least, make little sense. For example, I went to Glauco once to ask him where the Xerox machine was. He replied that one of the employees was assigned to run the Xerox machine and it would take forever to get something copied unless one was "a friend" of this employee. Glauco would take care of it for me. I could see some logic to this system; it supported and strengthened human relationships and friendships by (apparent) mutual aid. But it has serious drawbacks; it is inefficient, and in the case of science, it occasionally leads to the establishment of a scientific lab that is based more on these relationships than on the quality of the science. For example, years later, when I was on the Scientific Advisory Board to the institute, I learned of the factors that, in some cases, were involved in the evaluation of scientific programs. The evening before my very first meeting, where we would be examining the research proposal of a Doctor X, the director of the institute took me aside and explained: "X is the mistress of Professor Y at the University of Naples. This professor can be very helpful to us in certain negotiations with the university, so keep that in mind when we consider this program."

It was clear that this American-style institute still had to function in a culture with values and a social structure that clashed with the dream of Buzzatti. Yet despite all this, the institute flourishes.

The ironic, sometimes cynical view of life held by contemporary Neapolitans sprang from a long, unbroken tradition, according to the history books. So did the ancient custom of exchanging favors to get things done. It occurred to me that the creativity of the scientists I knew may have been in part due to the resourcefulness needed to survive in such a culture. Aspects of this culture reflect and underlie the power of the Mafia—or Camorra, as it is known in Naples. Nevertheless, the Neapolitan way of life had not prevented the city from becoming one of the three or four cultural centers of Europe, only a few centuries ago. Naples was renowned for its music, particularly opera, its literature, and its philosophy during the eighteenth century. The prominence of the city began to decline only with the changes that took place after the unification of Italy in the mid-nineteenth century.

My stay in Naples was as politically formative for me as my year in Paris had been. Experiencing a different culture influenced both my views of social change and my style of doing politics. These experiences made me realize just how hard it is to achieve social and cultural change. I had found myself attracted to many features of the Neapolitan lifestyle—features that seemed inseparable from cultural practices that had their dark side. I had not been used to such intensity of interpersonal interaction. It might be anger, it might be negotiation, it might be love or sex—but it was engagement. I asked myself: If you believe in political change, how do you retain the many positive features of a culture? How do you deal with centuries-old—or even millennia-old—cultural practices? Some of the hard dogmatic trends in left-wing politics that I had been attracted to began to appear less attractive.

Before leaving Boston I had considered more radical political ideologies. Friendly with the Harvard philosopher Hilary Putnam at the time, I found persuasive his arguments for the politics of the Progressive Labor Party, a Maoist group. Upon my return to Boston from Naples, I lost my interest in any kind of rigid political line. My brief period in Naples strengthened my questioning of simple solutions and awakened my need for a strong human element in my politics (and my science).

My stay at IIGB was also to have an important influence on the scientific directions I would follow in the future. I had been taking a genetic approach to biological problems for nearly ten years. We geneticists did not break open cells, extract proteins, and study reactions in the test tube to solve fundamental problems. Instead, we studied biological phenomena directly with the living bacteria.

Sydney Brenner, a died-in-the-wool geneticist, described proudly his great successes of the 1960s: "We did it all without ever touching the biochemistry."

Our path to understanding biological phenomena began with the isolation of mutations of an organism that were altered in the expression of some trait. We then "mapped" these mutations to locate them to a particular gene on a chromosome. We compared how the mutant and the wild-type (nonmutant parent) organisms behaved with regard to the trait. These comparisons often led to new biological insights. Many other genetic approaches have been developed over the years that have made such studies easier. The important point for us geneticists is that we are looking at an in vivo phenomenon—the behavior of the organism while it grows.

Since the founding of genetics at the beginning of the twentieth century, this approach has been used successfully to illuminate a host of fundamental biological questions. For example, the model for gene regulation proposed by Pardee, Jacob, and Monod was based on the isolation of mutations of E. coli. These mutations, in a gene named lacI, caused the organism to make the enzyme β-galactosidase all the time rather than only when the inducer lactose was present in the growth medium. When the researchers introduced these lacI mutations back into the wild-type lacI$^+$ bacteria, they created a bacteria that carried both the wild-type and the mutated gene. A comparison of the synthesis of β-galactosidase in these different bacteria led to the formulation of the repressor model of gene control. The Pasteur researchers had never broken open the bacterial cells and extracted a repressor molecule, nor, therefore, had they shown that the repressor could *directly* block expression of the β-galactosidase gene. Nevertheless, the genetic evidence they obtained was compelling enough to the scientific community for the PaJaMo paper to become an instant classic in molecular biology.

Inspired by the work of scientists such as Jacob, Monod, and Brenner, I had followed their path. In 1969, my colleagues and I obtained a new class of mutations that affected the ability of E. coli to make β-galactosidase—mutations very different from the promoter mutations we had isolated previously. The properties of the bacteria carrying these mutations suggested that a hitherto undiscovered factor was involved in controlling the lac genes. Our collaboration with the biochemist Geoffrey Zubay of Columbia University revealed that the mutations were in a gene coding for a protein essential for β-galactosidase synthesis. We named that protein CAP. (The name CAP stands for catabolite gene activator protein, reflecting its relation to the catabolism—digestion—of sugars by the bacteria.) The discovery of this new regulatory protein for the lac genes meant that the expression of the genes we had studied for so many years was more complex than we had previously thought. This novel feature of the lac genes, discovered simultaneously in the laboratory of Ira Pastan at the National Institutes of Health, was to be the last major aspect of the expression of the lac genes that would be discovered from genetic studies alone. Progress on the problem of gene expression—working out the details of the interactions between regulatory proteins and the DNA—would require biochemistry. If I were to continue studying the lac genes, I would have to become a biochemist again. This recognition was one of the factors that led me to choose Tocchini-Valentini's laboratory for my leave.

I would begin to do some serious biochemistry for the first time. Although I had been trained early in my career in chemistry and biochemistry, my interests and enthusiasm had moved so far over to the genetic side that I had little experience in the techniques that had developed in the intervening years. I planned to isolate more of the pure lac gene DNA using the technique that had brought my colleagues and me such attention. With a sample of

CAP protein obtained from Geoffrey Zubay, I would study in the test tube the interactions of CAP, RNA polymerase, and other proteins involved in expression of the lac genes with this DNA. The first step was to repeat the procedures outlined in the 1969 *Nature* paper—purify the two lac-carrying viruses and extract the DNA. With Bruno Esposito's help, I was able to obtain large amounts of the viruses. But then, when I tried to obtain pure preparations of the viruses, I was unable to separate them from other components of the bacterial extracts with the usual procedure of ultracentrifugation. I asked advice from everyone at the institute who knew anything about viruses, including Enrico Calef, the virus expert, who was visiting from Rome. I tried all suggestions. No one could explain my failure. I felt ridiculous. I seemed to have permanently lost my skills on the more chemical side of biology.

The failure to succeed at this very simple first step in my biochemical experiments was a shock. If I were to continue studying the lac operon—plumbing the details of how genes work—I would have to develop biochemical skills. I began to doubt whether I could make a success of the project. Perhaps I would have to think of different scientific problems to study where I could utilize my talents as a geneticist. The mental processes of genetics were now my forte and my love. I was confident that genetics could be used to approach any problem and that E. coli presented many other, often more complex fundamental problems that I could fruitfully study. I took time during my stay in Naples to read and think about new directions. It was there that I first began to consider studying the problem of protein secretion—how cells export certain of their proteins beyond the membranes that normally present an impassable barrier. I would initiate this project shortly after returning to Boston.

I switched back to genetics, working with Paolo on the project I had assigned him. We were trying to understand one of the promoter mutations John Scaife, Neil Krieger, and I had isolated years before. We were interested in the mutation because it not only inactivated the promoter site, but also inactivated the repressor that regulated the lac genes. In the short time I was there, the project did not proceed very far, but Paolo and I became good friends; the next year he would come to my lab as a postdoctoral fellow.

In December 1970, four months after we had arrived in Naples, our son Ben fell out of a tree and broke his arm. We could not find a doctor who could set it properly, so, at the advice of researchers at the institute, Barbara and Ben flew back to Boston and Children's Hospital. Since doctors in Boston wanted Ben to stay where they could keep an eye on his arm, Anthony and I followed shortly afterward. My important stay in Naples had lasted only four months.

CHAPTER 6

Does Science Take a Back Seat to Politics?

I wrote this book to make the case that a scientist can pursue a productive scientific career and still be a social activist within science. Many scientists believe that it is not possible. The eminent Yale biologist Clement Markert, who dropped the political militancy of his youth, said, "I made the conscious decision that I could not be both a first-rate scientist and a social activist." As I thought back on my career, I realized that there was a time when I too began to have doubts.

I returned from Naples at the end of 1970 still uncertain about what directions my science should take. In the next few years, my lab's scientific productivity declined. For the first time, the National Institutes of Health (NIH) gave my grant request a poor rating and reduced my funding. At the time, I felt I'd been treated unfairly. When I look back at the work my colleagues and I were doing during that period, I can understand why the NIH review committee was less than enthusiastic. Between 1972 and 1976, we published between one and two papers a year. In the previous four years, we had published an average of five research papers a year. These earlier papers were mainly the result of laboratory work carried out well before 1970.

My change in scientific directions provides a partial explanation for this decline. The failure at IIGB to succeed at elementary biochemistry forced me to think about new projects. Nevertheless, when Paolo Bazzicalupo came to my lab from Naples, we made one last attempt to do biochemistry—to study the lac genes in the test tube. We recruited a graduate student experienced in the study of isolated DNA molecules to assist us. Dean Hamer worked in the Biochemistry Department, close to our lab at the Harvard Medical School. Paolo and Dean worked for months trying to get our purified lac gene to function in the test tube, to make its product, the RNA that would encode the enzyme β-galactosidase. Nothing worked. We thanked Dean, who returned to his lab, and we moved on to another project. Now, there were no thoughts of continuing any biochemistry in the lab. We would concentrate on my strength—genetics.

Twenty years later Dean and I met again, but, this time as opponents in controversies over the relationship between genes and human behavior. Dean had become a researcher at the NIH, and had turned to studying the genetics of human sexuality. In 1993 he published a paper in the journal Science reporting that he had found a genetic marker on the human X chromosome associated with homosexuality in some males. I, in the meantime, had become a vocal critic of the poor scientific quality of studies in human behavioral genetics. I also questioned claims for the social significance of any findings in the field. Dean and I debated these issues in various meetings in the 1990s, including sessions of an advisory group to a publisher of high school biology curricula, and in a forum on behavioral genetics at Dartmouth University.

In addition to attempts to do biochemical experiments, much of the other work in the lab at this point consisted of cleaning up the details of ongoing projects. My colleagues and I obtained new classes of promoter mutations that interfered with the first step in expression of the lac genes—the copying of the genes' DNA into RNA. Our most important finding, however, came from the work of a graduate student in the lab, Malcolm Casadaban. Malcolm developed a new genetic technique that was to become essential for much of our work over the next several decades and would provide a major methodology for the study of biological problems in general. This technique, called gene fusion, entailed taking two normally unrelated and unconnected genes from the bacterial chromosome and joining them together so that they formed a single unit of expression. When we fused one gene to another, we eliminated the signals that normally regulated the functioning of one of the genes and placed that gene under the control of signals responsible for the expression of the other. For example, we used Malcolm's approach to connect the lac genes to the regulatory signals (for example, the promoter) of another set of genes. The products of this second set of genes (the ara genes) permitted the bacteria to grow on a sugar different from lactose that is called arabinose (see Figure 3). The ara genes are expressed only when arabinose is present in the growth media. When we fused the lac genes to the ara genes' promoter region, the bacteria no longer turned on β-galactosidase in response to the presence of lactose in the growth media, as they normally did. Instead, we had effectively tricked the bacteria into making β-galactosidase in response to the presence of arabinose in the growth media. The poor bacteria were wasting their energy doing this, because β-galactosidase is an enzyme of no use to the bacteria in their attempt to digest the sugar arabinose.

The important accomplishment was not the tricking of the bacteria. Rather, the gene fusion was useful for further studies because the expression of β-galactosidase was now an indicator of all the regulatory controls that ordinarily operated on the arabinose genes. Since β-galactosidase is a much easier enzyme to assay than the en-

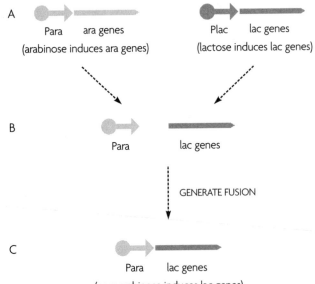

Figure 3. Fusing genes. A: The ara genes and the lac genes are normally distinct and separate from each other. They each have regions on the left in this diagram (Para and Plac) that ensure that they are properly regulated. B: By various kinds of genetic techniques, we can separate the lac or ara genes from their "P" regions. C: Then we can rearrange (fuse) these separated pieces of DNA so that one set of genes is regulated by a P region from another set of genes.

zymes involved in breaking down arabinose and since numerous genetic tools are available for analysis of the lac genes, all of these "lac" methods could now be used to study how the arabinose genes work. Currently, lac fusions to many different genes are used to study gene expression and other biological problems not only in bacteria, but also in many higher organisms, from yeasts to fruit flies to mice. The use of gene fusions such as these, along with gene cloning, polymerase chain reaction for amplifying small amounts of DNA, and DNA sequencing, has become one of the essential tools of molecular biology today.

In the meantime, I began exploratory experiments to follow up on the ideas for the project I had thought about in Naples. I designed genetic approaches to study the mechanism whereby bacterial cells can secrete proteins through their membranes. This new project eventually became the impetus for the resurgence of the science in my lab. The inspiration for studying protein secretion came from my departmental colleague Luigi Gorini. Luigi had a Ph.D. student, Mina Bissell, working on this problem, one that previously had essentially been ignored in the study of bacteria. Working with the rather obscure microbe *Sarcina*, she examined the mechanism that this organism used for exporting some of its proteins into the growth media. I saw this as a challenging biological problem, but one that could be better approached with the power of *Escherichia coli* genetics.

The early 1970s was a period of change in biology. For many years, molecular biologists had used bacteria as a tool for studying biological mechanisms. Now with the great successes and insights into the structure and function of chromosomes, into how genes work and into the metabolism that fuels the growth of cells, many scientists switched their laboratories over to work on organisms more complex than bacteria—fruit flies, worms, mice, and even humans. François Jacob has recently explained this period of change in biology: "If we didn't want to stand around rehashing the same old questions, we needed the courage to abandon old lines of research and old models, to turn to new problems and study them with more suitable organisms." But I felt that we had not even begun to touch the more complex problems of the biology of bacteria. Up to this time, molecular biologists had largely focused on how genes work, how the information encoded in the DNA is translated into the sequence and structure of a protein, how the expression of that information is regulated—the field that Pardee, Jacob, and Monod had opened up. In many cases, those who moved on to research with higher organisms still concentrated on these questions of gene expression. Yet this was not the only choice to make. It seemed to me that now was also the time to move on to more complex questions in bacteria themselves, for example, ones that dealt with the movement of proteins within the cell to different locations and even beyond the cell's cytoplasm— the movement of large molecules in three-dimensional space. This is where I felt that some of the imagination and "courage" in biology should be directed. I knew that it would be a long time before my research on protein secretion bore fruit. Changing projects was not an immediate solution to the slowdown in progress in the lab.

▲ ▲ ▲ This transitional period in biology and in my laboratory partially explains the decline in my lab's productivity. But there were other factors. The cultural and political turmoil of the late sixties and early seventies intruded into life in the laboratory. Some of those joining my lab group were students and postdoctoral fellows who were questioning their commitment to science, rebelling against convention, and considering alternate lifestyles. I have always run my laboratory with a relaxed hand. Perhaps some of this laxity was a consequence of my own hesitations along the path to becoming a scientist. I did not, like Art Pardee, have an idea—a model—for how to become a scientist. Therefore, I could not find it in myself to press people to behave in a particular way or even to work hard if they were not enthusiastic about the work. Lowell Hager had operated as a supervisor in much the same way. I could only hope that my enthusiasm and excitement for our projects would communicate itself. For those students who had serious questions about their future in science, I would cite the ups and downs of my own career. It may be that this relaxed atmosphere in the lab appealed to students who were the most uncertain about their future. Whatever the reasons, a number of people who chose to work in my lab were heavily involved in political or other counter-cultural activities.

Also, as I became well known for my political activities, some of the people who applied to work in my lab saw it as a place where they could comfortably combine their science and their political work. Donald Mikulecky is a case in point. Don had been doing research in another department at the Harvard Medical School. When he lost his position because of his political organizing among staff of that department, he sought refuge in my lab as a postdoctoral fellow.

Three postdoctoral fellows, Don Mikulecky, Rita Arditti, and Jim Shapiro, were active in Science for the People. One Ph.D. student, Michael Biales, left to go to art school after two years of thesis research. Another student, Richard Sanders, joined the Buddhist sect headquartered at the Naropa Institute in Colorado shortly after finishing his thesis in my lab. A third, Anne Gruyer, became deeply involved in Arica, one of the many guru-led counter-culture therapy groups. She would leave the lab soon after beginning her thesis work. Jim Shapiro left to teach science in Cuba not long after our press conference. (Jim did return to science after his sojourn in Cuba and is now a professor at the University of Chicago.)

Arthur Sussman, a postdoctoral fellow in my lab, made a change as striking as that of Jim Shapiro. I'd first met Art in 1970 in London at a conference on the social impact of biology; he made a strong impression, sweeping into the conference room wearing a long black cape. In my lab, Art's work went quite well; my fellow faculty members were impressed enough to offer him an assistant professorship in the department to pursue his own research. But within a few days of that offer, Art came to my office to announce that he was leaving science. He, his woman friend, and her child moved to northern California to live in a tepee. There, they changed their names to Sundance and Chiquita. While living in the tepee, Art wrote two books—*Handmade Hot Water Systems* and *The Brand New Testament*, a counter-cultural proposal for a new humor-infused religion—published by Joydeism [sic] Press. Then, in the

1980s, he returned to science, eventually working for a government-sponsored educational laboratory in the San Francisco Bay area. He has recently published the highly praised Dr. *Art's Guide to Planet Earth*, which received a special award from the California Science Teachers Association.

Despite such dramatic lifestyle and political changes in the lab, a few people, including the graduate students Susan Gottesman, Jeffrey Miller, and Malcolm Casadaban and the postdoctoral fellow William Reznikoff, were able to accomplish a lot during this period. We joked that Bill, who campaigned for George McGovern for President in 1968, was the conservative in the lab.

The influence of cultural changes was not limited to my lab. In my own department, I saw many other young scientists, students, postdoctoral fellows, and some faculty members experimenting with new lifestyles or political activism. Most of them have stayed in science and have had productive careers.

▲ ▲ ▲ In retrospect, it is clear that the transitional nature of my scientific research program and the societal influences on the people working in my lab must have played a major role in the slowdown in my research. Yet at the time I attributed this decline largely to my own growing political activism in science. When I returned from Naples, I was committed to following the political trajectory that had begun with our press conference. I wanted to focus my energies on the ways in which science influenced society. The organization Science for the People became the center of my political activity.

In the political atmosphere of the late 1960s and early 1970s, Science for the People attracted activists from many science-connected fields and professions. The early recruits were largely academics—faculty members and students—biologists, physicists, computer scientists, and a few chemists. As the organization rapidly grew, secondary school and college science teachers joined Science for the People, along with scientists working in technology-based industries, and others who had little scientific training, but who were alarmed at the consequences of scientific and technological developments. Members organized a session for the December 1969 meeting of the American Association for the Advancement of Science (AAAS) entitled "The Sorry State of Science." I saw this session on the local public television station and was stunned by the strength of the challenge presented. For the first time a major scientific conference featured significant discussion of the social impact of science. The young scientists decrying the misuses of science were seen by a wide audience.

Activist scientists formed chapters of Science for the People in cities around the country. including Berkeley, Madison, Chicago, New York City, Boston, Los Angeles, St. Louis, and Ann Arbor, Michigan. The Boston chapter proposed converting a newsletter of the organization to a bimonthly magazine. Science for the People magazine articles encompassed a wide range of issues reflecting the diverse nature of its members: the military uses of science, computers and privacy, the impact of U.S. policy on third world agriculture, genetic engineering, genetics and racial discrimination, science education, occupational health hazards, environmental problems, nuclear weapons and nuclear energy. This coverage of disparate issues worked because of the growing belief that many of the negative consequences of scientific and technological developments could be traced to questions of class and economics. The political events of the 1960s had increased the number of people generally dissatisfied with the political/economic system in the United States. An overarching critique that saw the political system itself as the major source of problems related to science and technology was appealingly simple. The dangers my colleagues and I worried about in our 1969 press conference—the potential misuses of genetics—appeared rooted in the same economic and social factors that led to the overuse of pesticides, the neglect of workplace safety, and the use of laser-guided weapons to kill Vietnamese.

A few months after my return from Naples, I joined the editorial committee for an issue of *Science for the People* magazine. I helped organize the Science Teaching Group within Science for the People (SftP) to develop a critique of science education. The members of this group were critical of the traditional presentation of science in schools as an objective, neutral pursuit. We saw that students, some of them future scientists, learned science without any reference to the cultural, social, and political influences on science and the social consequences of scientific developments. The typical science curriculum left out the harmful effects of science and technology and presented science as a smooth, inevitable, almost error-free progression toward the truth. Textbook writers ignored the roles of intuition, luck, and personal idiosyncrasy, all factors that give a more human face to the practice of science. Science emerged as a beneficent, yet almost sterile pursuit.

This distortion of the workings of science cheated students out of a realistic view of science that recognized both its personal and its social context. Science becomes something almost unfathomable and unchallengeable in its perfection. Future citizens were left ill prepared to question the significance of the scientific developments presented to them by the media—science that might affect their lives. Students who would become scientists were ill prepared by this education for any untoward consequences of the work they might do.

To reach science teachers with our critique, we organized workshops in the Boston area for teachers. SftP members from other parts of the country joined us to make presentations at the annual meetings of the National Science Teachers' Association and National Association of Biology Teachers. We prepared classroom materials to teach about issues such as IQ and race, genetic engineering, nutrition and world hunger, and environmental pollution.

I worked in groups that included high school science teachers, academic researchers and students, and scientists working in computer and other technology-based industries. This mix connected me with the day-to-day experiences of people in different work situations. Some of us picketed outside Polaroid Corporation buildings to support colleagues protesting labor conditions. Teachers in the group invited me to meet with their high school science classes. These experiences influenced my own teaching of graduate students. I incorporated examples of the social connections of science into my seminar class on bacterial genetics. When I handed out a set of research papers on the nature of mutations, I included articles on the presence of mutagenic and carcinogenic substances in industrial workplaces. My students read a well-known fraudulent genetic paper along with papers on the social and personal factors that influence scientific practice. An article on the history of the eugenics movement in the United States early in the twentieth century opened up discussions of scientists' responsibility for the consequences of their research.

Other SftP groups reached out to those segments of society that were benefiting the least from scientific progress. Members of Science for Vietnam, the New World Agriculture Group, the Technical Assistance Project, and other members who were examining occupational health issues offered their scientific and technical know-how to people at both the national and the international level. We protested military research on campuses and held our own conferences on campuses to highlight controversial issues.

In the early days, many of us in SftP looked to other societies as a source of inspiration for appropriate ways of utilizing science and technology. Members organized two Science for the People trips to China; those who went returned with glowing reports of conditions in the People's Republic. One of these trips took place in the midst of the Cultural Revolution! When the destructive consequences of this period in China became clear, I began to worry. I realized that I, like other members of the group, eager to find an alternative to U.S. society and its scientific policy, had been gullible. I had been enthusiastic about social policies in China after reading books such as William Hinton's *FanShen* and Dr. Joshua Horn's *Away with All Pests* that glorified the changes taking place in China. Although there were social programs that did help the Chinese population, many of us had been blinded to the disastrous and oppressive nature of China's policies by our desire to find examples of societies that were trying to serve all their people.

Later, Nicaragua became a beacon to leftists, including members of SftP. By this time, I was prepared to look at such beacons with a critical eye. Many of the members of the Ann Arbor SftP chapter spent extended periods of time in Nicaragua, assisting the government with agricultural matters. One of them, in articles for *Science for the People* magazine, presented the situation in that country as one of unalloyed progress. But in private letters to members, she described the shortcomings of the Sandinistas. This was a great disappointment to me. I felt that we should have learned that even if we are supportive of a social movement such as that in Nicaragua, we should also be open in our criticism when criticism is deserved. Not to do this was a disservice to our audience in the United States and also to the social movement that we supported. People came to feel duped when they learned that the situation in these societies was not as ideal as they had been led to believe. The result of this disappointment was often disaffection with activism itself.

When Barbara and I visited Cuba in 1984 and 1985, we both wrote articles, mine on science, hers on education, that pointed out the problems resulting from dogmatism and authoritarianism in Cuban society. At the same time, we pointed out those aspects of social policy that benefited Cuban citizens. In 1987, I published a letter in the progressive magazine *Mother Jones*, arguing that we should not offer simply "uncritical applause" for leftist revolutions such as that in Nicaragua.

Culturally and politically, SftP was a mix of conflicting tendencies. Its members included anarchists and Marxists, socially concerned scientific workers with no fixed ideological bent, and nonscientists who were strongly influenced by the counter-culture. Although many of us recognized both the beneficial and the destructive potential of scientific progress, some of the members appeared to be motivated by a general distrust of science. The tension between these different tendencies erupted in debates that punctuated periods of productive activity—anarchists against Marxists, scientists against those influenced by the counter-culture, women against men. To complicate matters, sectarian left-wing groups such as the October League and the National Caucus of Labor Committees attempted to flood meetings with their members and take over SftP. The October League did succeed in forcing the organization into a year-long debate in the late 1970s over their "Principles of Unity," a strongly Marxist-oriented document that they proposed should guide our actions.

I spent endless hours in meetings of a caucus of those of us who were opposed to such guidelines, meetings that continued for more than a year. We believed that if the October League was successful, Science for the People would become just another isolated, humorless mouthpiece for a quasi-religious dogma. Despite these internal contradictions, the frequently naive simplification of society's problems, and the long struggle to avoid dogmatism, a large number of committed activists kept the organization strong for many years. For most members, Science for the People was an essential connection to the world beyond our own workplaces.

SftP has had a lasting impact on the dialogue over science and its social impact. After the "Sorry State of Science" session in 1969, SftP regularly presented workshops, demonstrated, and petitioned at annual meetings of the American Association for the Advancement of Science. As a result, the AAAS began to incorporate sessions on science and social issues into its programs, a feature that continues to this day. Science for the People planted the seeds for many groups that influenced public debates on scientific issues. New organizations emerged out of SftP activity groups or were started by former members of SftP: the anti–nuclear energy Clamshell Alliance, local committees on occupational safety and health (COSH), the Committee for Responsible Genetics, and the Genetic Screening Study Group. Many SftP activists continue to teach courses and participate in projects that carry on its tradition.

In 1990, Science for the People suspended publication of its magazine because of financial problems and the waning political activism of the 1980s. I was asked to take on the presidency of SftP—the first time (and last) that we had a president—in an attempt to restore its finances. It was a losing battle. The organization disbanded, sapped of energy and incapable of raising the money needed to survive. I stuck with it until the end because there was no other group that placed the issues of science and society in a wider societal context. Also, it had been a part of my life for twenty years.

▲ ▲ ▲ There are ups and downs in the scientific life of any laboratory. Sometimes it seems as if nothing is working; at other times everyone seems to have the magic touch. Learning that these ups and downs are part of the life is a matter of survival for scientists. The period in my lab between 1972 and 1975 was one of these down times. I worried that my political activities were the main explanation for this slowdown—that the time I was devoting to Science for the People activities prevented me from concentrating suf-ficiently on advising my lab group.

Two graduate students, Lennie Guarente and Aparna Sarthy, came to me in 1972 and asked whether they could do their Ph.D. thesis work in my lab. I would be happy to have them, I said, but warned that because of my political commitments, I might not be the best advisor for them. Neither of these students was politically active, a harbinger of the arrival of the post-sixties generations. Nevertheless, they apparently still felt that the lab environment was attractive enough to take a chance on it. Both completed their Ph.D.'s in my lab. Lennie is now a professor at MIT and Aparna leads a research group at Abbott Laboratories.

The science in my lab did begin to gather momentum again around 1975. When this recovery began, my political involvement had not diminished. I would be able to continue to live these two lives.

Their Own Atomic History

This looks like any ordinary scientific session: a large lecture hall, several hundred scientists sitting with pens and notepads, the speakers on the stage waiting their turn. At the podium, Leilani Muir of Alberta, Canada, begins her presentation before the 1997 meeting of behavior genetics and neurobiology researchers in Orléans, France. Muir, however, is not a scientist about to report her recent results. Instead, she tells a more personal story, one that brings tears to many in the audience, even those familiar with the history of the eugenics movement. Leilani's experience lends a heart-rending reality to this shameful period in scientific history.

Muir cannot bear children. She was not born infertile. She was sterilized in 1959, at the age of fourteen. Muir describes her childhood: Her mother severely mistreated her, frequently tying her up and leaving her all day in their basement. Eventually the mother placed Leilani in a home for the mentally retarded, where, after scoring only 64 on an IQ test, she was certified a moron. That label allowed her to be legally sterilized under an Alberta eugenics law enacted in 1928. At the time, the teenager was told that she was being hospitalized for an appendectomy. She did not learn that she had been sterilized until thirteen years later when, at the age of twenty-seven, she sought an explanation for her inability to get pregnant. Muir recently took an IQ test again; this time her score was 101.

Judge William Baltimore of the United States follows Muir on the program, speaking on the relevance of behavior genetics to criminal law. I then describe the social impact of behavior genetics research on social policy during the twentieth century. Here I am, a bacterial geneticist, speaking to geneticists studying the behavior of everything from fruit flies to humans. And, I am lecturing to them about the little-discussed history of their own field. I have followed two citizens who talked about their personal experiences of behavior genetics in a social context. This is not the kind of forum scientists have come to expect at a scientific conference.

▲ ▲ ▲ More than two thousand Albertans were sterilized between 1928 and 1972 under the Albertan Sterilization Act. All were victims of the success of the North American eugenics movements early in the twentieth century. Until recently, few geneticists knew much about this movement, which flourished in the United States, Canada, and Europe. Fewer still realized that their own research field, genetics, played a significant part in the movement. In contrast to geneticists, physicists in the last half of the twentieth century openly confronted a historical burden from their past. They were forced by constant reminders to recognize the consequences of their role in the development of atomic bombs. In the decades following the dropping of the bombs on Hiroshima and Nagasaki, fears over the dangers of such weapons were kept fresh by the tensions of the Cold War. This weighty burden fueled a sense of social responsibility among many in the field. In the 1950s and the 1960s, physicists lobbied both the Congress and the public for greater control over these weapons. They published the widely circulated *Bulletin of Atomic Scientists*, in which they argued for peace, the cessation of nuclear testing, and the reduction of nuclear weapons. Physicists were prominent in the formation of the Pugwash organization, which organized conferences between U.S. and Soviet scientists, with goals similar to that of the *Bulletin*.

Geneticists had no such constant prod to remember an earlier era when the work of their predecessors and the ideas of genetics were used to destructive ends. In contrast to the physicists, the geneticists were essentially ignorant of their own "atomic" history. I did not become aware of the eugenics movement until I was more than thirty-five years old. As a graduate student in chemistry and biochemistry, I audited a genetics course where there was no mention of the eugenic period. Nor did I ever hear about it in any of the genetics labs I passed through. When I returned to Harvard in 1965, I stocked my shelves with textbooks on genetics and microbiology, none of which made any mention of the eugenics movement.

It was not until the early 1970s that I came across a book that opened my eyes to this history. I read a book review in *Science* entitled "A Tormented History." The reviewer praised *Genetics and American Society*, by the physician and historian of science Kenneth Ludmerer. The book documents the rise of the eugenics movement and the role of geneticists in that rise. I borrowed the book from the Harvard Medical School library; fascinated by this hidden history, I read through it within a couple of days. I learned of the behavior of scientists during the genetic movement and how scientific ideas from genetics were converted into social policy. Reading Ludmerer's book and other writings on eugenics has had an enormous influence on me. Much of what I have done since as an activist within science I attribute to my own recapture of this history.

Eugenics movements were evolving more or less in parallel in the United States and Western Europe. The origins of the movement in the United States are complex. The major eugenics organization evolved from an association concerned mainly with cattle breeding and was led by men from the upper social classes. Eugenicists believed that human social traits and aptitudes were inherited. With the rediscovery of Mendel's laws of inheritance at the beginning of the twentieth century, eugenicists realized that they had a powerful new scientific tool to support their program. They claimed that the quality of the gene pool in the United States was deteriorating. They called for policies that would increase the number of people with "good" genes and decrease the proportion of the population that carried "defective" genes. Prominent aristocratic figures in the eugenics movement such as Madison Grant, author of the popular eugenics book *The Passing of the Great Race*, and Robert DeCourcy Ward, a leader of the Immigration Restriction League, used the new genetic concepts to support their claims for the inferiority of certain ethnic groups and the lower social classes.

In the first two decades of the twentieth century, most of the leading geneticists were seduced by or promoted eugenic theories. According to Ludmerer, every member of the first editorial board of the journal *Genetics* (founded in 1916), Thomas Hunt Morgan, William E. Castle, Edward M. East, Herbert S. Jennings, and Raymond Pearl, had given support to the eugenics movement. Pearl stated, "I doubt if there is any other line of thought or endeavor on which common international discussion and *action* can be so well and so profitably brought about as with eugenics." East (who ultimately showed that many traits were determined by multiple genes) felt that without eugenics "man's troubles will speedily multiply as they never have before." Michael Guyer, another leading geneticist, worried that "our very civilization hangs on the issue [eugenics]." Genetics textbooks, written by eminent geneticists such as Harvard's Castle, included sections on eugenics. Three quarters of all colleges and universities in the country offered courses that were devoted entirely to eugenics or that included sections on eugenics. Eugenics was considered a respectable scientific discipline.

Despite this respectability, the methods of the new "science" of eugenics fell far short of the standards used in the rest of genetic research. Take the case of Charles Davenport, head of the Eugenics Record Office at Cold Spring Harbor, Long Island. The Harvard-trained geneticist had done careful studies on the pattern of family inheritance of Huntington's disease. He deduced correctly that the disease was exhibited by individuals who had a mutation in only one of their two copies of the "Huntington's" gene. Huntington's disease was due to a "dominant" mutation. Yet Davenport also claimed that social phenomena such as criminality, poverty, intelligence, and even seafaringness could be attributed to single genes. His conclusions on Huntington's disease were based on a precise description of the disease and careful examination of family pedigrees. Davenport supported his claims for inheritance of personal behaviors and aptitudes by citing poorly defined traits and questionable pedigrees. His conclusions appeared to reflect little more than his own prejudices. Davenport also argued with even less evidence that reproductive intermingling of different racial and ethnic groups would lead to inferior progeny.

As I read through Ludmerer's book, I tried to understand why so many scientists promoted eugenic theories, given the weakness of the underlying science. One explanation, I thought, was the very successes of genetics following the rediscovery in 1900 of Mendel's laws of inheritance. The early years of the twentieth century witnessed a series of remarkable advances; one after another simple trait was shown to follow Mendelian rules. From Mendel's pea plants, to traits of the fruit fly *Drosophila*, to human genetic disorders such as alkaptonuria and Huntington's disease, the concept of single gene determinants held sway. This unquestionably powerful new theory and analytic tool may have generated an overweening confidence among geneticists; they came to believe that the same simple genetic concepts could explain more complex human traits. When a successful new theory appears, scientists often extend its explanatory power to account for a wider range of phenomena than it can handle. As the scientific field matures, scientists eventually come to agree on more modest applications of the theory.

However, it is unlikely that the prevalence of eugenics thinking among geneticists is explained simply by their ambition to proclaim an all-encompassing theory. Ludmerer points out that the leading geneticists of this period came mainly from the upper social classes, descendants of early American ancestors. The early years of the twentieth century were a time of considerable social turmoil in the United States. Disruptive labor strife and major immigration movements were changing the social and ethnic fabric of society. Unhappy with these changes, those who supported eugenics sought the roots of social phenomena in the genetic defects of individuals or of the disdained ethnic groups. Eugenics presented not only an explanation, but also a solution: restore the ideal genetic makeup to society. It must have been soothing to those in the upper echelons of society to be able to attribute society's problems to the immigrants and poorer sectors of society. Rather than having to surrender any privilege, this class could look instead to eugenics as a solution.

Conservative social attitudes cannot explain all the various strands of the eugenics movement, however. Margaret Sanger and other liberal and left-wing figures supported eugenics programs in the belief that they would, in fact, benefit the poorer members of society. Eugenics ideology was also strong among socialists in Germany and among Communists during the early years of the Soviet Union. In some cases, these attitudes of left-wing political figures may have been consistent with their own class origins. Many of them came from bourgeois or even upper-class families.

The eugenics movement, a social and political force with an apparently scientific base, significantly influenced public policy in the United States. The push for eugenics programs yielded state and federal legislation that profoundly affected many people's lives. A majority of states passed laws that allowed sterilization of people who had low intelligence, or who exhibited certain kinds of criminality and other behavioral "abnormalities." Supporters of these laws cited the claims of eugenicists that the traits meriting sterilization were genetically determined. Like Leilani Muir and others in Canada, tens of thousands of people in the United States were sterilized under these laws. Many states also passed laws forbidding marriage between individuals of different races, miscegenation laws that relied on "scientific" theories of the inferiority of hybrid "races." The U.S. Congress passed the Immigration Restriction Act of 1924, which dramatically reduced the number of people allowed into the country from southern and eastern Europe and from other cultures considered inferior. Eugenicists and psychologists who had given IQ tests to immigrants testified before congressional committees in support of this bill.

I became interested in the process that allowed such damaging legislation to pass so readily. It appeared to me that the development of popular attitudes toward eugenics was an important key in generating the atmosphere that made such legislation possible. Members of the eugenics movement communicated their views to the public in many ways. They presented displays at county and state fairs explaining the ideas of eugenics, often illustrating them with dramatic pictures of families with "superior" and "inferior" genes. They taught courses on eugenics in colleges and universities. They fostered eugenic ideas in the popular press. I looked back at popular magazines and newspapers of the day and found articles that promoted genetic explanations of societal problems: "Decadence of Human Heredity," "Plain Remarks on Immigration for Plain Americans," and "Danger That World Scum Will Demoralize

America." The *National Geographic* in 1918 devoted an entire issue to "The Races of Europe," which included a characterization of different ethnic groups according to their supposedly hereditarily based "racial" behavioral traits. This flood of propaganda helped strengthen eugenic attitudes among the public.

I wanted to see how a widely read science magazine of the day had treated the subject. I chose *Popular Science Monthly*, edited by the respected psychologist James McKeen Cattell. I spent afternoons in the basement library of Harvard's Cabot Science Center, leafing through issues. A sampling of eugenics-oriented articles from the magazine, written mainly by scientists, shows the influence of the movement on popular culture. In the years 1913 through 1915, *Popular Science Monthly* published articles with the following titles:

"Going through Ellis Island"

"A Study in Jewish Psychopathology"

"Heredity and the Hall of Fame"

"The Biological Status and Social Worth of the Mulatto"

"Heredity, Culpability, Praiseworthiness, and Reward"

"Eugenics with Special Reference to Intellect and Character"

"Immigration and the Public Health"

"A Problem in Educational Eugenics"

"Economic Factors in Eugenics"

"The Racial Element in National Vitality"

"Eugenics and War: The Dysgenic Effects of War"

"Families of American Men of Science"

"Biological Effects of Race Movements"

A few excerpts give a sense of this "popular science." In the report on "Jewish psychopathology," Dr. J. G. Wilson argued that "Jews are a highly inbred and psychopathically inclined race" and that "among the frankly feeble-minded, the Jews stand next to the top of the list of those immigrants who are deported on that account." David Starr Jordan, evolutionist and president of Stanford University, in the "Biological Effects of Race Movements" spoke of the "lower races" that were immigrating into the United States from Europe and Asia and lowering "our own average." Dr. H. E. Jordan of the University of Virginia in "The Biological Status and Social Worth of the Mulatto" cited the geneticist Charles Davenport and the statistician Karl Pearson in concluding that "negro traits (e.g. cheerful temperament, vivid imagination . . .) are of the nature of unit characteristics [i.e. due to single genes]."

The eugenics movement had moved from academic theorizing to communication to the public via the media and other means and, finally, with the desired public attitudes generated, to the enactment of social policy.

As the field of genetics matured, many geneticists who had supported eugenics in the United States gradually withdrew their backing. The increasing sophistication of genetics made clear just how complex human genetics could be. Nevertheless, the falling off of scientific support had little influence on the implementation of eugenics policies. Eugenicists were well mobilized and active in their political efforts. In contrast, the recently disaffected geneticists rarely went public. By the time they spoke out against the policy proposals of the eugenicists, it was too late. The geneticists East, Castle, and Jennings only criticized the eugenically based Immigration Restriction Act at the last minute before its passage by Congress. Despite their increasing disdain for the scientific arguments of eugenics, geneticists were generally silent. Thomas Hunt Morgan, the most prominent geneticist of the day, became very critical privately of the genetic arguments underlying eugenics. He explains his reluctance to publicly confront the social consequences of these arguments in a private letter to a colleague written in 1915: "If they [eugenicists] want to do this sort of thing, well and good . . . but, I think it is just as well for some of us to set a better standard, and not appear as participators in the show. I have no desire to make any fuss" (cited by Garland Allen in "Genetics, Eugenics, and Class Struggle"). Geneticists generally stayed away from the fray, even though they recognized the harm that was being done. By 1924, with the enactment of the Immigration Restriction Act, most of the legislation eugenicists had sought had become law.

After 1924, the eugenics movement began to fade in the United States. But in Europe its impact was only beginning to be felt. In 1923, Adolf Hitler attempted his famous beer hall putsch. Having escaped arrest, he hid in the house of his close friend, the publisher Julius Lehmann. When Hitler was finally caught and imprisoned in 1924, Lehmann sent him a book recently published by his press. In jail, Hitler read passages such as the following:

> "Fraud and the use of insulting language are commoner among Jews."
>
> "In general, a Negro is not inclined to work hard."
>
> "The Mongolian character . . . inclines to petrifaction in the traditional."
>
> "The Russians excel in suffering and in endurance."
>
> "In respect of mental gifts the Nordic race marches in the van of mankind."

The authors of this book also stated:

> What historians regard as degeneration, sickness and ageing of a nation, what they look upon as the decline of a nation, are the outcome of a reversed selection of the racial constituents of the people concerned.

Today, these claims read like excerpts from a Ku Klux Klan or Aryan Nation publication. But they aren't; they appear in one of the most widely used human genetics texts of the time, *Human Heredity*. Its authors were the German geneticists Erwin Baur and Fritz Lenz and the German anthropologist Eugen Fischer. They were not second-rate scientists. Lenz had been the first to show a relationship between consanguinity and the manifestation of recessive genes. Baur discovered the first lethal gene. Eugen Fischer, after an illustrious career, was appointed rector of Berlin University. *Human Heredity* used genetics as a way of making respectable the characterization of races and ethnic groups according to their genetically based personality traits. The book was practically a manual of eugenics and biological determinism. Writing in the late 1990s, the German geneticist Benno Müller-Hill argues that the sections of Hitler's *Mein Kampf* dealing with human genetics and eugenics read as though they were directly influenced by the claims he found in *Human Heredity*.

As I continued to read *Human Heredity*, I encountered more surprises. Hardly anywhere in this text did I find the authors' arguments to be supported by any German scientific research. Rather, their main source of data and argumentation came from the scientific establishment of the United States. The book is replete with tables and pedigree charts from the likes of the psychologists and intelligence testers Lewis Terman and Edward Thorndike and from U.S. geneticists such as Charles Davenport.

I had first learned of the text *Human Heredity* in 1973 from a Harvard undergraduate student, Robert Waldinger. He had written an undergraduate honors thesis entitled "The High Priests of Nature: Medicine in Germany, 1883–1933," based on research he had done in Germany. Through a friend, Waldinger had heard of my interest in eugenics and he lent me a copy of his honors thesis. From Waldinger's thesis, I also learned that those Germans who promoted eugenic social policy (or "racial hygiene" as it was termed in Germany) often based their arguments on the American science of eugenics and on U.S. eugenics legislation. In 1923, a leading German physician urged the federal government to obtain copies of U.S. sterilization laws and begin their implementation in Germany:

> What we racial hygienists promote is not at all new or unheard of. In a cultured nation of the first order, in the United States of America, that which we strive toward was introduced and tested long ago. It is all so clear and simple.

The 1907 sterilization law enacted in the state of Indiana became the model for the first German eugenic sterilization programs. The German racial hygiene movement, begun well before the Nazis took power, derived some of its inspiration and its respectability from what had already happened in the United States. The impact of the eugenics movement in the United States and of the geneticists who had supported it had moved far beyond the country's shores.

Among the writings that detail the role of German geneticists and doctors in the eugenics policies of Nazi Germany, those of Benno Müller-Hill are the most striking. Müller-Hill's 1988 book *Murderous Science* exposed to German society for the first time just how deeply involved its scientists and doctors were in planning and supporting the sterilizations and elimination of millions of people. I first met Benno in the early 1960s at the Institut Pasteur during one of my attempts to find a place in François Jacob's lab. Benno, who was there on a scientific visit, made a strong impression on me. He seemed to me to be one of those young scientists who had been attracted to molecular biology because of the new science itself and because of the more liberal culture in the field. I was wearing jacket and tie, still the common dress among academic scientists. Benno was wearing Levis and a denim work shirt, which, unusual then, later became almost a uniform for molecular biologists. A few years after this meeting, I was back at the Harvard Medical School and Benno was a postdoctoral fellow with Walter Gilbert at the Harvard campus in Cambridge. We became friends, and often talked politics and marched together in Vietnam War protests.

Benno and I also had much in common scientifically. During one of the anti–Vietnam War marches, our talk turned to science. I told him about my lab's success in cloning the lac genes into bacterial viruses. These viruses turned out to be exactly what he had been looking for to pursue his studies on the repressor of the lac genes. He and Wally Gilbert had isolated the repressor, the first time a regulatory protein had been obtained in the test tube. They would use the DNA extracted from my lab's viruses to show that the repressor acted directly on genes themselves. Their work eventually yielded direct biochemical proof of the Jacob-Monod theory of gene regulation.

Because Benno and I shared so much both politically and scientifically, we kept in touch after he left Boston. In 1970, Barbara and I and our two sons visited Benno in Cologne, where he had taken a faculty position at the university. Although we still talked both politics and science, neither then nor in our many meetings afterward did we ever talk about the social impact of genetics. Only when Benno began writing his book did I learn that we had shared a mutual interest in the historical basis of eugenics for all those years. My surprise at learning that the two of us had developed common concerns about the interaction of genetics and society was much like my reaction to finding that my former labmate, François Williams, and I had converged in many of our views. In each case, during the years we had known each other, the subject never arose. Discourse among scientists simply did not include discussions of the social impact of science.

Publication of *Murderous Science* in Germany, even in 1988, was a courageous act. Many of the scientists complicit in the Nazi era were still alive and influential in German universities. Müller-Hill became persona non grata among much of the genetics community in Germany. His book, widely reviewed in other countries, was not even covered by German newspapers or journals. It was not until 1999 that the German scientific establishment began to explore the role of scientists before and during the Nazi era. Partly because of Benno's prodding, scientific institutes have initiated the release of old files documenting the activities of scientists suspected of being complicit in Nazi atrocities.

The extreme misuse of genetics, first by German scientists and then by the Nazi government, drove some prominent English and U.S. geneticists to speak out more openly. At the seventh International Congress of Genetics in 1939, a number of them issued a "manifesto" criticizing eugenic programs. The signers included J. B. S. Haldane, J. S. Huxley, H. J. Muller, Theodosius Dobzhansky, and A. G. Steinberg. Several of these geneticists, while they held eugenics views themselves, were appalled by the implementation of eugenics in Germany. For the most part, however, the opposition of geneticists to the misapplication of their field was too little and too late to have any effect.

The universal postwar revulsion at the Nazi eugenics policies led to a rejection by geneticists and others of many of the general tenets of the eugenics movement. In particular, the position that human behavioral traits and social problems were largely genetic in origin was replaced by the position that environment was the determining factor in such issues. Some of these positions are presented in two statements issued by UNESCO in the early 1950s. One of the statements, prepared by leading physical anthropologists and geneticists (several of them from the group that wrote the 1939 statement), criticized the concept of race and argued that differences in culture, intellectual achievement, and behavior between ethnic groups were not genetic in origin. A few geneticists, notably Th. Dobzhansky, continued to be outspoken about the misuses of genetics in the next decades.

To my mind, the history of the eugenics movement in the United States should be essential reading for geneticists. Knowledge of this history is instructive not because there is likely to be a repeat of anything resembling the horrors that occurred in the United States and Germany. Rather, understanding the role and behavior of geneticists during the eugenics era may influence our actions in the face of a new era of genetic advances. Why did so many leading geneticists adhere to eugenics concepts in those early days? Why did they fail to speak out publicly against eugenics and its legislative agenda once they had become disaffected from the movement? Were they aware of the impact of U.S. eugenic scientific research and conclusions on the budding racial hygiene movement in Germany and on Nazi policies? How is it that physicists developed a social conscience in response to Hiroshima and Nagasaki, while geneticists quickly forgot about the consequences of these misapplications of genetics? The damage done by eugenic legislation in the United States and the horrors of the Holocaust may still have occurred without the participation and, later, the silence of geneticists. But who knows what the impact would have been if significant numbers of socially conscious members of the genetics community had early on expressed their indignation at the misuse of their field?

At the 1969 press conference, my colleagues and I had expressed fears about the consequences of our work. At this very beginning of my concerns about the impact of genetics, I wondered how, as scientists, we could prevent the progress of science from causing harm to people. I questioned whether geneticists should be in the business of creating better and better techniques for manipulating the genes of human beings, given their potential abuses. Did the risks of pursuing this science outweigh its benefits? Perhaps I should oppose the development of these techniques. Jim Shapiro had expressed these same concerns when he chose to leave scientific research. The advent of recombinant DNA technology, the surprising genetic breakthrough of the early 1970s, heightened the dilemma for me. Human gene manipulation was close at hand. I had not settled these questions for myself even as late as 1977. At a National Academy of Sciences forum on recombinant DNA, I publicly questioned whether the genetics community should proceed at all with recombinant DNA research.

But as I read of the history of eugenics, I began to take a different view. The eugenicists were successful in pushing for the passage of sterilization, miscegenation, and immigration restriction laws because they were able to convince the public and legislators that heredity was the explanation for society's ills. The idea that people's worth to society could be assessed by the nature of their genes became accepted wisdom. I realized that it was not the scientific development of the technique of sterilization that rendered Leilani Muir and hundreds of thousands of others infertile against their will or without their knowledge. The misappropriation of science grew out of a combination of factors that had nothing to do with a medical procedure that could be used either to benefit or to hurt people. The harm done was the consequence of scientific studies that presented a view of genetics as deterministic of people's fates in life. These studies were flawed by the social biases that the scientists brought to the research they were doing. Scientists, others in the eugenics movement, and the media presented these distorted representations of genetic theory and genetic science to the public with the prestige of science behind them. In a society where questions of social disruption, crime, and immigration were prominent, these ideas were rapidly accepted and translated into social policy. Finally, the failure of those geneticists who were critical of this science to speak out gave eugenicists free rein to claim the authority of science for their ideas.

I still worried about society's ability to foresee and forestall the negative consequences of certain new scientific advances. Yet I realized that the potential for such consequences will always exist, as long as we do not confront all the other factors that lead to the misuse of new technologies. I saw that even today the kinds of biological determinist scientific arguments that eugenicists had made early in the twentieth century are being repeated, albeit in different forms. Scientists and the media once again are attracting attention to claims of genetic bases for criminality, poverty, and racial differences in intelligence.

I slowly changed my position. I became convinced that stopping a scientific development did not even necessarily prevent the feared misuse. The scientific lines of research that lead to specific new technologies are often unpredictable. We might halt one line of research only to find that the ability to manipulate human genes rapidly has emerged from some other research area. In the meantime, we would not have confronted the ideology, the faulty science, and the communication of that misconceived science to the public that made the feared misuses possible. I also knew that stopping a scientific line of research might prevent potential intellectual and practical benefits. So I decided to concentrate on the ideological stances that fueled the misuses of scientific developments, rather than on opposing new developments in genetics because of their potential negative consequences. I would work on reaching the public and my scientific colleagues with "exposés" of socially loaded claims masquerading as objective science. In my teaching, writing, and public speaking, I would try to restore to geneticists a historical memory of their "atomic" era. I hoped that the awareness of scientists themselves and of an informed public would create sufficient force to ensure more beneficial uses of science.

▲ ▲ ▲ The recapturing of history has consequences. In 1996, Leilani Muir won a suit against the province of Alberta for her invol-
untary sterilization. In 1998, following Muir's lead, nearly five
hundred people, two thirds of the surviving victims of sterilization
in Alberta, successfully claimed compensation. The remaining suits
are still in litigation. The public exposure of Muir's travails revealed
the role of a prominent psychologist, Dr. John MacEachran, in her
case. MacEachran, who was head of the Department of Philosophy
and Psychology at the University of Alberta in Edmonton, was also
head of the board that ordered the sterilization of Muir and many
others. Protests, including those of scientists, led to the psychologist's name being removed from an honorary lectureship and an
important meeting room at the university.

CHAPTER 8

The Myth of the Criminal Chromosome

Sigourney Weaver lies unconscious in the wreckage of her downed space capsule. She is the only survivor of the Alien attack and has crash-landed on the planet Fury 161. A particularly unsavory looking set of characters comes to her rescue. These are the "double Y chromos," men who, instead of the usual single male Y chromosome, carry a double dose of male-determining genes in all their cells. Their two Y chromosomes doom them to lives of criminal, antisocial behavior. Since there is no hope of rehabilitation for these genetically determined perverts, the rulers of Earth have exiled XYY males to a distant uninhabited planet. Weaver is facing, according to their leader, a collection of "thieves, murderers, rapists and child molesters . . . all scum." She must survive not only the Alien, but also this untrustworthy band of deviants.

The myth of the XYY male may have reached its popular apogee in the science fiction film *Alien 3* in 1993, but it had begun to take hold as far back as 1965. In that year, the publication of a short genetics research paper on the subject attracted widespread media attention. Now, more than thirty-five years later, the public (and the makers of *Alien 3*) still have not learned that the scientific community had largely rejected the image of the XYY male as super-criminal by the mid-1970s.

▲ ▲ ▲ In 1973, my chance meeting with a young psychiatrist from Boston's Children's Hospital put me right in the middle of the debates over XYY males and criminal behavior. At an anti–Vietnam War meeting, Dr. Herbert Schreier introduced himself to me and described an XYY research project at his hospital that he felt was unethical. The director of the study, the psychiatrist Stanley Walzer, was interested in studying the behavioral consequences of the XYY genotype. Dr. Walzer began by screening newborn baby boys for the extra Y chromosome at the Boston Lying-In maternity hospital. He then asked parents of the boys if they would be willing to join a project in which he would follow the behavioral development of the children. As Herb and I examined the details of the study, we became convinced that it had serious scientific and ethical problems. We decided to challenge this project before Harvard committees, since both the Children's and the Lying-In hospitals were affiliated with the Harvard Medical School and Dr. Walzer was a Harvard faculty member. The controversy that followed led to a severe conflict with my colleagues on the Harvard faculty and threatened to end my tenure as a Harvard professor.

I was by now primed from the reading I had done in the history of eugenics to be suspicious of genetic research that purported to explain antisocial behavior. I had learned of the various ways that flawed studies on genes and criminality had been translated into misguided social policy. The genetic basis of criminality and antisocial behavior was a central tenet of the eugenicists. The psychologist H. H. Goddard, popularizer of the Binet IQ test in the United States, published a report in 1912 describing the pseudonymous Martin Kallikak, who sired children by two women, one feebleminded and the other a person of "high quality." According to Goddard, most of the former woman's children and grandchildren showed varying degrees of antisocial behavior, while all the latter woman's descendants were of good moral character. Influenced by these and other such reports, legislators passed laws in the early part of the twentieth century that allowed sterilization of criminals. Goddard's contentions found their way into psychology textbooks, some of which, well into the 1950s, featured cartoonish sketches of the families of Martin Kallikak as evidence for the genetic basis of bad behavior.

However, by the 1960s, despite its long shelf life, Goddard's study of the Kallikak's was no longer considered scientifically reputable. A final blow was delivered by Stephen Jay Gould when he published evidence in his book *The Mismeasure of Man* that Goddard, attempting to strengthen his case, had even doctored photographs of the families that appeared in his report. In the new era of molecular biology and with the availability of more sophisticated genetic techniques, scientists did not find persuasive those studies that showed that criminality ran in families. What was required as proof was something more biological, something observable in the laboratory in human samples—a genetic marker that could be correlated with criminal acts in an individual. By this time, microscopy techniques had improved to the point where researchers could accurately observe and count the full complement of chromosomes in human cells. These improvements led to the discovery that Down Syndrome patients and individuals with certain other physical or mental problems carried extra chromosomes.

The XYY male made his dramatic appearance within a few years of the development of these new chromosome visualization techniques. Dr. Patricia Jacobs and her colleagues in Edinburgh, Scotland, published an article entitled "Aggressive Behavior, Mental Subnormality, and the XYY Male" in the December 25, 1965, issue of the journal *Nature*. The research group reported a study of inmates of a special security prison in Scotland who were said to be "mentally sub-normal." They used the new microscopy techniques to search for extrachromosomal material in these males. The geneticists, wondering whether "an extra Y chromosome predisposes its carriers to unusually aggressive behavior," focused their attention on this male-determining chromosome. They found that 7 out of 197 inmates (3.5 percent) were XYY males. The authors suspected a causal relationship between the extra Y chromosome and the incarceration of these men, because of this apparent high frequency. The provocative title of the *Nature* paper reporting the study generated widespread interest among geneticists. Other researchers attempted to replicate Jacobs's findings. Surveys in prisons failed to yield high frequencies of XYY males. However, a few screenings performed in institutions for the criminally insane turned up results like those reported in the first paper. A firestorm of publicity ensued.

In the United States, articles appeared in magazines and newspapers with titles such as "Genetic Abnormality Linked to Crime" (*New York Times*, April 21, 1968), "The XYY and the Criminal" (*New York Times*, October, 20, 1968), "Chromosomes and Crime" (same title in *Science Digest*, December 1967, and *Psychology Today*, October 1968), and "Born Bad?" (*Newsweek*, May 6, 1968). A dramatic crime in the United States aroused even more public interest. In 1968, claims appeared that a famous mass murderer, Richard Speck, was an XYY male. Late one night in 1966, Speck had entered an apartment where Chicago nursing trainees lived and killed eight of the students. Convicted of the crime, he filed an appeal in 1968. At that point, a well-known geneticist in Philadelphia, Mary Telfer, suggested to a *New York Times* reporter that Speck was an XYY male. After all, he was tall, had severe acne, was somewhat retarded, and had killed people, all characteristics consistent with what was "known" about XYY males. The *New York Times* reported Telfer's claims and, a day later, reported that Speck's chromosomes had been examined and that he was indeed an XYY male. This report was false, a result of miscommunication between the *Times* reporter and a doctor in Chicago. The *New York Times*, however, never corrected the original claim. A geneticist, Eric Engel, who had already found that Speck exhibited the normal XY chromosome composition, did not announce his findings publicly to rebut the newspaper reports. He revealed them only in 1972 in an obscure scientific journal. The public, never having learned of this error, would only remember that Richard Speck was an XYY male. Nationwide, Americans came to associate the XYY male with horrendous crimes.

Why did Dr. Engel never publicly refute the reports that Speck was an XYY male? Could it be that, like Thomas Hunt Morgan during the eugenic era, he did not want to "appear as [a] participator in the show?" One scientist did come to regret her role in this circus. Patricia Jacobs, who had started the firestorm with her 1965 paper, much later (1982) expressed her dismay at the fall-out from the presentation of her work: "In retrospect, I should not have used the words 'aggressive behavior' in the title of my paper and should not have described the institution as a place for 'the treatment of individuals with dangerous, violent, or criminal propensities.'" This is an interesting admission. For it raises the question of why she had used those words in her title in the first place. The simplest explanation is that the title reflected a strong assumption underlying her study—that a double dose of the Y chromosome meant a double dose of male aggressiveness. Even though they were aware of the public representations of the XYY story, neither Dr. Engel nor Dr. Jacobs spoke out to correct these misconceptions. They chose not to confront the social consequences of this science.

And consequences there were. The "myth" of the XYY male entered the realm of public fact. Medical school psychiatry tomes and high school biology texts presented the XYY "syndrome" as scientific truth. A section of a widely used medical school psychiatry textbook (by Alfred M. Freedman, Harold I. Kaplan, and Benjamin J. Sadock) on the genetics of criminal behavior was dramatically illustrated with a photograph of Richard Speck. In England, a popular spy novel, *The XYY Man*, was made into a television series. The 1971 Italian movie *The Cat O'Nine Tails*, directed by the prominent horror movie director Dario Argento told the story of a serial murderer who kills to keep his XYY chromosomal makeup secret. In the United States, the states of Maryland and Massachusetts established screening programs to detect XYY males among imprisoned juvenile offenders. XYY prisoners were treated with female hormones to reverse their apparent super-maleness. As late as 1993, the myth of the XYY male was alive and well when *Alien 3* appeared on movie screens. Even today, the majority of students in my genetics classes know the XYY story and most believe that the link between the extra Y chromosome is scientifically established.

Yet criticisms of XYY science had appeared soon after Jacobs's first publication. Researchers reported that XYY males found in institutions tended to be taller than the average, scored lower than average on intelligence tests, and often suffered from severe acne. The incarceration of these individuals might easily have been related to these factors rather than to supposed super-aggressive genes. Taller men might be more likely to be apprehended than those of average height. The severe acne or the lower intelligence of XYY boys might well have affected their interactions with their peers and have generated any antisocial attitudes they might exhibit. Moreover, as researchers looked closely at the behavior of the incarcerated XYY males, they found that these men had usually committed crimes against property rather than against people and were less aggressive than other inmates.

Other scientists pointed to the absence of control groups for the studies of men in prison settings. There were no reports indicating the proportion of XYY males in the general population, and no studies comparing the behavior of noninstitutionalized XYY males with those in prison. These failings exemplify a problem that has, in the past, plagued genetic studies of human disease and behavior. Genetic abnormalities are usually discovered only when those who suffer severe health or developmental problems see a physician. But these same genetic abnormalities may exist in other people who suffer no or very mild consequences from their altered hereditary material. Since those without symptoms never see doctors for their particular problems, doctors never see them. As a result of relying on their observations of the patients that they do see, physician-researchers have tended to assume the worst-case scenarios, concluding that the presence of a particular genetic marker inevitably led to the more extreme forms of a disease. XYY researchers had made a similar error. They had examined individuals in penal institutions, found a high frequency of XYY males, and proposed a correlation between the extra Y chromosome and criminal behavior. They made this suggestion without knowing anything about XYY males outside of such institutions.

Today, scientists are far more sophisticated about the degree of correlation between a genetic mutation and the manifestation of a disease or trait. The recent explosion in the development of genetic screening techniques is largely responsible for this change. Now, as scientists and doctors readily detect specific disease mutations in families or in the general population, they are finding that, for many diseases, there is not a one-to-one correlation between mutation and disease. For instance, cystic fibrosis is usually associated with a profound disease of the lungs and with infertility. However, of two males carrying the same mutations for cystic fibrosis, one may be severely disabled and die at an early age, and the other may only exhibit infertility.

In fact, a parallel situation exists with XYY males. As researchers began to study XYY males in the general population, it became clear that the frequency of males born with an extra Y chromosome was itself high; approximately 1 in 1,000 males had the extra chromosome. This means, for example, that there are over 100,000 XYY males in the U.S. population. Only a tiny fraction of these men could be in prison settings. The major scientific review of literature in the XYY field concluded in 1974 that "the frequency of antisocial behavior of the XYY male is probably not very different from non-XYY persons of similar backgrounds and social class." In 1976, a group of Danish researchers led by H. A. Witkin published a study in *Science* that put to rest the XYY myth for many scientists. Their study examined the behavior of tall XYY males from the general population and found that they were not "especially aggressive." Until then, no one had attempted to characterize the behavior of XYY males other than those found in penal institutions. More recent studies of this sort report some degree of learning disability among XYY males, but no indications of aggressive or violent behavior.

The XYY myth captured the imagination of the American public at a time of increasing public concern about violence. The faulty scientific studies and the overwrought response to them may have been more a social phenomenon than a scientific one. The Democratic administration of the early 1960s had introduced the War on Poverty, a set of programs designed to alleviate societal problems by remedying adverse social conditions. The problems had not gone away. Richard Nixon was elected in 1968 partly because he promised to be "tough on crime." Genetically based criminality provided an explanation, comfortable to many, for a discomfiting social problem. If criminals were "born bad," then perhaps the only solutions were tough penal measures and genetic screening, not increased spending on improved recreational facilities for inner-city teenagers or antipoverty programs. The Center for Studies of Crime and Delinquency of the National Institute of Mental Health, founded in 1966, supported a number of XYY research projects, including Dr. Walzer's study. The proposal that genes explained criminal behavior paralleled Arthur Jensen's claims in 1969 that the failure of blacks in the education system was due to their inferior genes. In both cases, social problems that might require changes in social policy were attributed to people's genetic makeup. Jensen's genetic explanation for poor school performance was taken to mean that there's nothing society can do about it. Right-wing congressmen entered Jensen's 1969 article into the *Congressional Record* in support of attempts to end compensatory education programs.

The history of XYY research represents a classic case of how things can go wrong when scientists study issues of social import. The researchers treated this very complex human behavioral issue simplistically and rushed to conclusions based on flimsy data. They lent a sensationalist turn to their science with provocative titles and conclusions. The cachet of objective science lent an aura of truth to their claims, resulting in uncritical media reporting. The media amplified the implications of the scientific reports, influencing the attitudes of the public and policy makers. Even when scientists recognized the fall-out from their work, they failed to correct the public misimpressions. Left uncorrected, these misimpressions were translated into public polices such as genetic screening programs in prisons and increased funding for the study of the genetic roots of crime.

Furthermore, the scientists and the media often presented the XYY story as though these men were doomed to lives of aggressive, antisocial, and criminal behavior. Even if the evidence had been strong that an extra Y chromosome contributed to antisocial behavior, these reports should have been tempered with the acknowledgment that genetic does not mean doomed or fated. Human traits influenced by genes may also be strongly influenced by nutrition, family upbringing, economic conditions, and other cultural and social factors. Some genetic diseases can be treated and sometimes cured, for example by changing the individual's diet. In addition, the genetic basis of the disease itself may be complex, involving the effects of many genes that vary from person to person. If the XYY constitution does somehow increase the propensity to aggressiveness, this does not mean that every male with an extra Y chromosome or even most males with it will exhibit the behavior. But "fated," "doomed," "inveterate," "born bad," and "congenital criminals" were the words used to describe the imagined XYY male. This misguided genetic determinism still influences the presentation of much of genetics to the public today.

▲ ▲ ▲ It was this knowledge of the history of XYY research that piqued my interest when Herb Schreier told me of the study at Children's Hospital. We invited other scientists, mostly from the Harvard Medical School, to join us in our analysis of the newborn screening program. Our group included Luigi Gorini, Jonathan King, a geneticist from MIT, and Richard Roblin. Roblin, in that same year, 1973, was one of the cosigners of the letter from scientists, including Jim Watson and Paul Berg, who proposed a moratorium on recombinant DNA research. We began to look into the nature of the study, how parents were recruited, and how Dr. Walzer hoped to determine the consequences, if any, of the XYY genotype. (Walzer was also following the development of XXY males, boys with an extra X chromosome.) We discovered that hospital staff members asked women for permission to analyze the chromosomes of their newborn baby boys at their most vulnerable moment, as they entered the maternity hospital in labor. The prospective mothers then signed a short, misleading informed consent form that told them that "if any serious abnormalities are found, you will be so informed." When an extra X or Y chromosome was detected, Dr. Walzer would contact the parents, telling them of the uncertain consequences of the "abnormality," saying that he would like to follow the development of the child and offering help if behavioral problems arose. Jay Katz of the Yale Law School, a well-known authority in the field of ethics in experimentation, wrote to me that he found the consent forms used "elements of 'fraud, deceit,' and even 'duress and overreaching,' proscribed by the Nuremberg Code" (letter of September 30, 1974).

If this study had not been preceded by the Jacobs study and the years of publicity, it would have been much less problematic. But by this time, the popular conception of the XYY male had influenced both the design of studies of this sort and their potential impact on the families involved. Much of the public had come to believe that XYY males were "born bad." Walzer, not wanting to raise the anxiety of the parents, never mentioned XYY in the consent forms or when he asked the parents if they would participate in the study. However, many parents in the study, knowing of the prior research, asked Walzer if the chromosome abnormality was XYY. He felt obliged to answer them honestly. Parents probably worried enough when they learned that their child carried an extra chromosome that might cause aberrant behavior. Imagine the increased concerns of those who "knew" that the child could show violent or even criminal tendencies. They "knew" this not because Dr. Walzer had told them. They were already well aware of the public image of the XYY male. Later, one of the mothers from the study contacted me, when our criticism of Walzer's research became widely known. She described how she and her husband had found themselves sensitive to any apparent indications of misbehavior on the child's part. The nervousness described to me by this mother was unlikely to be the only such case. In another similar study, a mother "admitted to anxieties about disobediences and rebellious behavior that, had she not known of the abnormality and its possible implications, would have otherwise caused her no concern."

It is difficult to know what influence parents' "knowledge" of the effects of the XYY genotype might have had on their behavior toward the child and on the child's development. On the one hand, they might have acted so as to successfully prevent further problems. On the other hand, their treatment of the child and their obvious nervousness might have induced a self-fulfilling prophecy. The very behavior they feared may have been the result. Further complicating family dynamics was the fact that the parents devised cover stories to explain to their neighbors why a child psychiatrist was making regular visits to their home—cover stories necessitated by the public's impressions that XYY males were violent.

Walzer's intervention in the children's development by offering help to parents if problems arose also raised scientific questions. What conclusion should he draw if the children showed no profound behavioral abnormalities? Would such a finding mean that the extra chromosome had no influence on behavior, or had he successfully prevented any serious problems by his intervention? Alternatively, what conclusion should he draw if a child did show antisocial tendencies? Was the behavior due to the extra chromosome or had the parental knowledge influenced the child's upbringing? Even Dr. Walzer acknowledged in his grant application for this project that "unless there is significant pressure from the parents, we do not divulge the specific nature of the extra chromosome material, since we feel that such information [that a child is XYY] could be detrimental to the child's psychological development." From a scientific point of view, it is hard to see how this study could yield results that anyone with a slightly critical eye could accept.

Finally, federal guidelines required scientists doing research with human beings to make a strong case that the benefits of their study outweighed the risks. But if our critique was correct, there were no clear-cut scientific benefits to this XYY study; Walzer's interventions in the families may have so influenced the development of the children that no conclusions could be drawn about the consequences of the extra chromosome. At the same time, the families' participation in this research entailed risks, possibly affecting negatively the upbringing of the child and the family environment. In theory, it was reasonable to determine whether an extra chromosome might cause behavioral or physical problems. But the history of XYY research complicated this type of study, perhaps beyond repair.

Our group filed a detailed complaint in March 1974 against the Walzer study with the Committee of Inquiry at the Harvard Medical School. This committee forwarded the complaint to the Committee on Medical Research, headed by Dr. Dana Farnsworth, one of the elder statesmen of the Harvard Medical School. Dr. Farnsworth invited Dr. Walzer, me, and others to testify at a meeting in the fall of 1974. At the meeting, members of our group were surprised to find how sensitive Dr. Walzer was to many of the problems we raised, and how eager he was to find ways to overcome them. However, subsequently, the committee met to question only Dr. Walzer; we were not invited. After its final meeting in November, Dr. Farnsworth reported to the Harvard Medical School faculty that the committee had voted to support the continuation of Walzer's study. But this turned out not to be the whole story. After Farnsworth's presentation, one of the committee members, Dr. Frank Speizer, approached me with unexpected information. Speizer told me that a majority of the committee had been quite dismayed by the XYY study and had actually voted to require such strict guidelines of Walzer that he was sure to discontinue the screening. Dr. Farnsworth offered his own strong views, suggesting that an end of this study would be a blow to academic freedom, and insisted on a revote. Faced with their chairman's stature and his dire warnings, the committee members revoted, with a majority now favoring continuation of the study without modification. In his final report, Farnsworth noted only that "several Committee members [worried] that the possible risks of the study might outweigh the benefits."

Our group became convinced that Farnsworth's actions indicated a determination by the administration of the Medical School and influential senior faculty members to support Walzer's study. In the same way that the Medical School administration had kept us at bay in committee meetings at the beginning of the Mission Hill housing controversy, the committee in this case seemed to have been simply a mechanism for validating the status quo. A majority of members of the investigating committee had at least initially agreed with our criticisms. We concluded that the process had been distorted. We called a press conference to announce and criticize the results of the Farnsworth's committee's deliberations. At the same time, Jonathan King and I published an article in the British journal *The New Scientist* entitled "The XYY Syndrome: A Dangerous Myth." In it, we reviewed the history of XYY research and described our challenges to the Walzer study at the Harvard Medical School.

We publicly rejected the report of the Committee on Human Studies and insisted that the issue be discussed and brought to a vote at a meeting of the full faculty. At a meeting of the faculty on March 14, 1975, we offered a resolution to reopen the review of Walzer's study. Professor David Potter of the Neurobiology Department and I spoke to support the motion and Drs. Park Gerald and Julius Richmond from Children's Hospital spoke against it; our resolution was rejected by an overwhelming majority of the faculty. After the meeting, a senior faculty member revealed to me that he and a group of other faculty members, angry with our actions, had been meeting to decide on a course of action. For this group, my worst sin was to bring in-house Harvard business before the public. They had considered going to the dean of the Medical School to request that my tenure be removed. With the overwhelming defeat of our resolution, the group now felt that such an action would no longer be necessary.

I was surprised at the strength of the vote against our attempts to halt this study. Many who had supported me in my critique of Harvard's neighborhood housing policies a few years earlier now strongly opposed our critique of the risks involved in a scientific study. I asked some of them whether they disagreed with our evaluation of the study. The responses I got revealed a deep concern among these scientists that I had not considered. One of them said to me, "If you can stop this scientific study, mine might be next." These colleagues looked on the halting of this scientific study as a violation of scientific freedom in general. But from our point of view, scientific freedom clearly has its limits in situations where people might be harmed. This study, we felt, violated human studies guidelines and, thus, under those guidelines, should not be continued. The whole point of human studies guidelines is to modify or prevent studies that might cause harm to people without their consent and with no balancing benefits. This was not the only reason for the lopsided vote. Some of the faculty members who did not have tenure told of being discouraged by senior members of their departments from voting for our resolution. However, I was bolstered by support from Howard Hiatt, dean of the Harvard School of Public Health and David Baltimore, a leading figure in cancer research at MIT.

The Harvard XYY controversy affected my personal life and psyche more than any other controversy I have been involved in. For the first and last time in my life, I suffered severe migraine headaches. I felt or imagined hostility from other faculty members as I passed by them in the halls of the Harvard Medical School. This distrust reached its height when my wife was found to have a growth on her thyroid gland. She was operated on by a Harvard

Medical School surgeon during the height of the controversy (December 16, 1974), three days after I had given a speech criticizing the study before the Harvard faculty. I worried: If this man is as hostile as some of the other faculty members, could he subconsciously take less care when operating on Barbara? Years later I was treated by the very same doctor and finally realized how ridiculous my fears had been. He was a jolly, genuinely friendly man who did not even remember the controversy. Nevertheless, my fears at the time highlight the intensity of the feelings this controversy generated.

The vote at the Harvard Medical School did not end the XYY controversy. Media attention attracted outside groups that wanted to look into the study. The Children's Defense Fund issued a critique of the newborn screening program, citing the harm it might do to the children. A representative from the Massachusetts Attorney General's Office visited Children's Hospital to investigate the study. As a result, Dr. Walzer announced in June 1975 that he had decided to stop the screening. He would continue to follow the children of families he had already engaged in the study. This resolution seemed reasonable to my group, since these families had already made the commitment and were seeing Dr. Walzer regularly; it seemed possible that, at this stage, disrupting this relationship could itself cause problems for the families. Similar programs to screen newborn baby boys for the XYY chromosomes were halted in Colorado and England, although we never learned of the reasons for these decisions. Eventually the Boston XYY controversy led to the establishment of a major project of the Hastings Center for Bioethics on ethical issues in genetic research.

Months after the end of the XYY controversy, a friend of mine was sitting in a bar in South Boston. Lying on a seat next to him was a copy of a Ku Klux Klan newspaper, *The Crusader*. My friend picked it up, opened it to an inside page, and there found a picture of Jonathan King and me. Under the picture, the caption, headlined "Reds Attack Genetic Research," said:

> Loudmouth Communist groups such as "Science for the People," have successfully prevented a research project in Boston which linked human genes to behavior. The obvious features of the Communist on the right leaves no doubt that these Bolsheviks are nothing more than the stormtroops of the Judeo-Liberal establishment."

The "Communist on the right" was me and the "features" referred to my obvious Jewish heritage. The picture had been reprinted from a *Newsweek* article on the Harvard controversy. Despite the virulent language in the caption, I was less disturbed by this attack than I was by the antagonism of my colleagues at Harvard. It was more upsetting to have people I met and interacted with daily harboring unexpressed resentments.

▲ ▲ ▲ In 1993, eighteen years after the end of the XYY controversy (and the year of *Alien 3*), I received a call from Dr. Xandra Breakefield, a Harvard Medical School researcher at Massachusetts General Hospital. She was disturbed by the way the media had reported on her recent research papers. Collaborating with a Dutch group led by Dr. Han Brunner, she had found a mutation associated with apparent aggressive behavior in men from a Dutch family. Her papers, one of which was published in *Science*, attracted the attention of television and newspaper reporters. Media reports suggested that this new genetic finding could explain everything from gang warfare in U.S. cities to the Arab-Israeli conflict. A lawyer in Georgia who was requesting a retrial of a man convicted of murder asked Dr. Breakefield if she would testify. The lawyer wanted to claim that a genetic propensity to aggression ran in his client's family. She asked me for advice on how to handle this situation ethically. I read the *Science* paper and came to the conclusion that she and her coauthors had perhaps inadvertently led readers to the interpretation that the media had seized upon. The paper ended with suggestions of a possible extension of the results to explain aggression in society more widely.

I was bemused by Dr. Breakefield's call. Twenty years before, I had been overwhelmingly and bitterly rejected by my colleagues for my critique of the genes and criminality study, and had almost lost my position at the Harvard Medical School. Now, in 1993, I was regarded by another faculty member as a source of ethical wisdom on the subject. Was this simply a result of a failure of the faculty's long-term collective memory? Had I changed? Or were the ethical issues I had brought up in the 1970s now considered mainstream?

The reactions of Dr. Breakefield to the media coverage of her study do indicate some change in the sensitivities of scientists. She and Dr. Brunner eventually dissociated themselves from the media representation of their work. Dr. Breakefield publicly announced that because the media seemed unable to handle such a subject in a reasonable way, she would not work on the subject of genes and aggression again. Dr. Brunner modified the conclusions of the paper, stating at a symposium on genes and criminality that "our studies have been repeatedly quoted as evidence for an aggression gene. This concept is unlikely to be productive and . . . is not in keeping with data as they were reported."

Drs. Breakefield and Brunner had shown more significant and timely concern for the social consequences of their work than many others had in the past. Their response contrasts with those of Drs. Engel and Jacobs, who, in the midst of a media blitz about the XYY male, did nothing to counter the impressions being relayed to the public. Nevertheless, the obvious surprise of Drs. Breakefield and Brunner at the hoopla accompanying the publication of their papers shows how little prepared they were to consider the social implications of what they do. They appeared to have no conception that their hints at broader implications of their work would be seized upon by the media in the predictable way that it was. Without a knowledge of the history of interactions between genetics and society, scientists will continue to see history repeat itself.

It's the Devil in Your DNA

TV weatherman Bill Murray awakens to the sound of his alarm clock radio. It's *Groundhog Day* in Punxsutawney, Pennsylvania. Puzzled, Murray realizes he is listening to the same music and the same radio chatter he heard the previous morning. He gets dressed and descends the stairs of the country inn only to meet the same person he had met the day before, saying the same things. With every step he takes, yesterday's events repeat. Each night he goes to bed, hoping that the next day will be a new one, only to wake again to the same chatter, the same conversations, the same occurrences. Murray is permanently stuck in Punxsutawney, endlessly repeating Groundhog Day. He tries every means he can think of, including suicide, to escape this nightmare.

On May 28, 1975, some of us woke up, read our daily *New York Times*, and reacted with Bill Murray–like puzzlement. But this was not a movie. In a front-page article, the *Times* science reporter Boyce Rensberger announced the upcoming publication of *Sociobiology: The New Synthesis*, by the Harvard professor E. O. Wilson. The *Times* story, titled "Sociobiology: Updating Darwin on Behavior," declared: "sociobiology . . . carries with it the revolutionary

implication that much of man's behavior towards his fellows, ranging from aggressive impulses to humanitarian inspirations, may be
as much a product of evolution as the structure of the hand or the
size of the brain." According to Rensberger: "Dr. Wilson said he
thinks sociobiology is leading to a view of man as being under the
influence of inherited 'programs of behavior that are more strict
than many psychologists would have us believe.'"

Here we were again, awakening to a new day, only to find ourselves reading the same old headlines—listening to the same old
"chatter." It was only two months after the end of my role in the
XYY story, and I was about to enter into yet another controversy
over genes and human behavior. The word "sociobiology" was
new to me. I couldn't imagine what kind of science would provide
such all-encompassing information about human social arrangements as the article promised. Rensberger's description of sociobiology made it sound like a modern version of earlier theories,
with features of the Social Darwinism of the nineteenth century
most prominent among them.

I had learned to be skeptical of scientific reports that claimed
new insights into the genetic basis of human behavior and aptitudes. My antennae were way up. I knew how complicated it was to
separate out the genetic, environmental, and cultural factors that
contribute to human behaviors. I knew how complicated it had
been for researchers to separate out their own cultural and social
attitudes from their investigations of the social behavior of others. I
knew of the sometimes frightful consequences that followed from
the misrepresentation of genetic knowledge.

Sociobiologists based their explanations of behavior on studies
of social organisms ranging from ants to apes. Grounding their rea-
soning in biological evolution, they developed theories such as
"reciprocal altruism" and "kinship selection" to account for the
behavior of animals toward each other. These new theories offered

satisfying explanations for many social phenomena in the animal kingdom. They were often testable by direct observation and the ability to manipulate populations of certain species. Although Wilson drew on anthropological, psychological, and sociological research on human societies, evolution was the bedrock of his analysis of human behavior.

Thus *Sociobiology: The New Synthesis* offered much more than an explanation of why there is male dominance among baboons or "rape" in scorpionflies. According to Wilson, the years of work on other animals now yielded explanations for a range of human social behaviors, including altruism, aggression, homosexuality, racist attitudes, the sexual division of labor, and class structures. Unlike earlier piecemeal efforts of scientists to find genes for IQ, criminality (or even seafaringness), sociobiology, as presented by Wilson, offered the awesome promise of an integrated, comprehensive approach to understanding the genetic basis of human societies. Sociobiology employed mathematical and population genetic theory (that is, hard science) to model and explain animal behavior and human social arrangements. Sociologists, psychologists, anthropologists, and others who had traditionally studied human behavior would have to change their approaches. Biology was about to absorb these "soft sciences" and make them "hard." The ascendant ambitions of sociobiology extended to other disciplines; according to Wilson: "Scientists and humanists should consider the possibility that the time has come for ethics to be removed temporarily from the hands of philosophers and biologicized."

The *New York Times* article on Wilson's book launched a media feeding frenzy that continued for the next several years. Popular interest emphasized the social implications of this new science. Stories first appeared in major newspapers, then in popular venues such as *People, Cosmopolitan, Playboy, Time* (a cover story), *Reader's*

Digest, and *House and Garden*. The media coverage made public figures of Wilson and other academics whose research was included under the umbrella of sociobiology. Radio and television talk shows were eager to interview these scientists. In October of 1975, Wilson offered a précis of his "synthesis" in a *New York Times Magazine* article entitled "Human Decency Is Animal." He began with a discussion of the evolutionary basis of altruism and then presented sociobiological explanations for homosexuality and the division of labor between the sexes. Although recognizing the role of cultural evolution and environmental factors, Wilson nevertheless went on to state:

> Thus, even with identical education and equal access to all professions, men are likely to continue to play a disproportionate role in political life, business, and science. But that is only a guess and, even if correct, could not be used to argue for anything less than sex-blind admission and free personal choice.

Overall, the media presentation gave the impression that there had been major new scientific insights into the genetic (evolutionary) influences on human behavior.

Given the impact of past theories of this sort, it seemed to me that those of us who were alert to this history should take a close look at the scientific basis of sociobiology. Shortly after the appearance of the *Times* article, I decided to check my reactions with Richard Lewontin, a Harvard University evolutionist and one of the few scientists who had been publicly critical of biological determinist thinking. He had been a student of the similarly outspoken geneticist Th. Dobzhansky. Dick was particularly active in pointing out the scientific fallacies underlying claims for genetically based racial differences in intelligence. He had also been a member of Science for the People since his days at the University of Chicago. What's more, Dick worked in the same building as E. O. Wilson and was quite familiar with sociobiology. He told me that Wilson had talked for some time of launching a major new effort to establish genetics and evolutionary theory as a basis for explaining human societies. Dick was skeptical of these claims, as he had been of earlier genetic theories of human behavior.

We agreed to call together a few people who might share our concerns. We would meet to consider whether and how to respond to this public surfacing of sociobiology. Toward the end of July a small group of us gathered at my house in Cambridge. We sat out on the breezy front porch, escaping the heat of a hot summer night. By this time, our own heat had mounted as sociobiology garnered increasing publicity for its claimed social implications. We decided to read Wilson's book and evaluate the scientific basis of its arguments. Dick pointed out that sociobiological explanations of human behavior incorporated studies from a range of academic disciplines. If we were to make sense of Wilson's arguments, we would need people in our group from these disciplines. We contacted others in the Boston area whom we knew would have a critical perspective on such theories: the paleontologist Stephen Jay Gould, the biologist Ruth Hubbard, the anthropologists Tony Leeds and Lila Leibowitz, the population biologist Richard Levins, and the psychologist Steve Chorover. We reached out as well to other academics, members of Science for the People, and some of those who had been involved in the XYY and recombinant DNA controversies. The group eventually grew to include high school teachers, psychologists, philosophers, anthropologists, psychiatrists, physicians, and students in college and graduate school. We took on the name the Sociobiology Study Group, and affiliated ourselves with Science for the People.

In the meantime, my wife, Barbara, then a high school teacher, discovered a biology curriculum used in her school that included an Educational Development Center module developed by the Harvard sociobiologists Robert Trivers and Irven DeVore. *Exploring Human Nature* presented sociobiological theory as though it were established fact. Phrases such as "scientists have concluded" were used throughout to preface sociobiological theories. Used in over a hundred school systems in twenty-six states, the text asked students, "Why don't females compete?" "Why aren't males choosy?" The authors posed these questions in a context which assumed that such presumed universal behaviors had an evolutionary explanation. The students were asked to look at the world around them and explain various social behaviors in terms of their evolutionarily adaptive significance. Barbara joined the Sociobiology Study Group.

Our second meeting took place in early August 1975. Many of us had now read the first and last chapters of Wilson's book—those that focused on the implications of sociobiology for human societies. Over the next few months we met regularly every two weeks, continuing to read and discuss chapters of the book. We were probably the first "book club" to choose Wilson's tome to read. Ironically, the sheer numbers in the group—as high as thirty people at some points—most of whom bought a copy of Wilson's book, made a contribution to the book's impressive early sales. We pinpointed flaws in the approaches of sociobiology and began to work out a critique. The wide range of expertise in the group allowed us to learn of examples from animal behavioral and anthropological studies that appeared to contradict many of the sociobiologists' claims.

As we saw the media coverage of the supposed social implications of sociobiology continue to grow, we became increasingly eager to publish a critique of *Sociobiology* in a journal that would reach a wide audience. The *New York Review of Books* had published a favorable review of Wilson's book. We decided to submit our critique as a response to the review. Several people wrote drafts, with

Stephen Jay Gould's version becoming the basis for group discussions and revisions. Our letter, signed by the then current sixteen members of the group, appeared in the November 13, 1975, issue of the New York Review of Books.

We prefaced our criticisms of Sociobiology: The New Synthesis with a short account of the history of biological determinist theories. The bulk of our letter, however, catalogued the scientific flaws that we felt undermined Wilson's attempted synthesis. We argued that he chose which behaviors were adaptive or maladaptive according to his own social views. He ignored cultural evolution as an equally reasonable explanation for much of human behavior or finessed the issue by attributing the course of cultural evolution to the genes. Furthermore, his use of anthropomorphic terms such as homosexuality, courtship, promiscuity, and xenophobia to describe animal behaviors allowed him to smoothly move to the same level of explanation for the behavior of humans as sociobiologists used for other animals. His reconstruction of human prehistory, which was crucial to his account of human evolution, was based on questionable extrapolations from physical anthropological studies and from studies on contemporary tribal cultures. Anthropologists had long differed over the interpretation of such studies.

In effect, we argued that the scientific support for the sociobiology of human behavior was weak and that its assumptions and choices of examples were influenced by a particular social view of the world. We concluded that "Wilson joins the long parade of biological determinists whose work has served to buttress the institutions of their society by exonerating them from responsibility for social problems."

The introductory account of biological determinism in our letter described the history of biological theories of human behavior and their consequences. We ended this section with the statement: "These theories provided an important basis for the enactment of sterilization laws and restrictive immigration laws by the United States between 1910 and 1930 and also for the eugenics policies which led to the establishment of gas chambers in Nazi Germany." The next paragraph began: "The latest attempt to reinvigorate these tired theories comes with the alleged creation of a new discipline, sociobiology." It was this passage that aroused the most ire not only among sociobiologists, but even among many who were otherwise willing to listen to our scientific criticisms. To introduce into a debate that should remain academic a juxtaposition of sociobiology and a science that was used as a rationale for Nazi policies seemed terribly unfair.

We did not think it was unfair. But we had, perhaps, become too familiar with the history of biological determinist theories. We failed to recognize that most people, even academics, were unaware of how eugenics, a science that had flourished most vigorously in the United States and had been supported by, among others, Harvard professors of the day, came to have such enormous social impact both in the United States and Germany. Eugenicists had spoken with certainty of their scientific conclusions and offered society prescriptive advice—which was heeded. We saw sociobiologists moving from speculation about human behavior to suggest to the public that there were limits on what changes in social arrangements were possible. The parallels seemed self-evident to us, if not to others.

The sociobiologists' theories that accounted for differences in sex roles attracted the most public interest. Like Wilson in his *New York Times* piece and later in his book *On Human Nature*, other sociobiologists explained behavioral and achievement differences between men and women according to evolutionary theory. David Barash, in his book *Sociobiology and Behavior* (1977), said: "Ironically, mother nature appears to be sexist." "Sociobiology explains why women have almost universally found themselves relegated to the nursery while men derive their greatest satisfaction from their jobs."

Wilson had become so well known by 1977 that the publishers apparently felt that Wilson's fulsome praise on the back cover of the paperback version of Barash's book was the only blurb necessary to ensure sales.

There were public consequences of the statements of Wilson and others about sex roles. Barbara, who later left teaching to become a journalist, surveyed popular magazines to see how they handled the sociobiological representation of this subject. In a 1984 article in the *Columbia Journalism Review*, she reported that magazines such as *Cosmopolitan* (1982–1983), *Playboy* (1978–1982), *Reader's Digest* (1982), and *Science Digest* (1982) breathlessly reported, sometimes in a series of articles, how this new science explained the world around us. *Playboy* referred to sociobiology in an article entitled "Darwin and the Double Standard" as a "new science [that] shows why men must cheat on their women." The magazine offered advice to its male readers: "If you get caught fooling around, don't say the devil made you do it. It's the devil in your DNA." On the basis of studies of "rape" in mallard ducks and scorpionflies (Barash reported that "rape is epidemic among mallard ducks"), rape in humans was treated as a natural male imperative in sociobiological publications. Therefore, not surprisingly, popular magazines picked up these explanations. *Playboy* stated that rape was "genetically based . . . a strategy genetically available to low-dominance males that increases their chances of reproducing and making females more available to them than they would otherwise acquire." *Psychology Today* and *Science Digest* repeated arguments about the "genetic programming" of rape in men.

A 1976 television film produced in Canada, *Sociobiology: Doing What Comes Naturally*, based on interviews with Wilson, Irven DeVore, and Robert Trivers, also placed its strongest emphasis on sex roles. The film showed human couples engaged in heavy petting and male baboons fighting over females, as the narrator argued that sociobiology puts the lie to the goals of the women's liberation movement. Trivers epitomized the ambition of the sociobiologists when he said in the film, "It's time we started viewing ourselves as having biological, genetic, and natural components to our behavior. And that we should start setting up a physical and social world which matches those tendencies." Such statements reflected the belief of many sociobiologists that their science would ultimately be important for the development of social policy. Our group showed the film during a forum at the Harvard Science Center. The imagery in "Doing What Comes Naturally" was so outrageous that Wilson, DeVore, and Trivers were forced to disown the film and ask that it not be distributed. Nevertheless, they stood by all the comments they made in the interviews. They apparently considered that the imagery in the film vulgarized their comments, but this vulgarization appeared to us to flow directly from their account of the conclusions of sociobiology.

It was perhaps this public face of sociobiology that led the philosopher Philip Kitcher to label the speculations about human behavior "pop sociobiology." In his 1985 book, *Vaulting Ambition: Sociobiology and the Quest for Human Nature*, Kitcher distinguished this aspect of sociobiological endeavor from the animal and insect studies, for which he had more respect.

With my attachment to France, I became interested in whether "pop sociobiology" had attracted the same attention in Europe as it had in the United States. I found that in England and France, where the women's movement was less prominent, interest in sociobiology centered on its discussions of class and race. The xenophobic, anti-Semitic National Front in England had used genetic claims of U.S. scientists even before sociobiology's arrival to argue that "the most important factor in the build-up of self-confidence among racists and the collapse of morale among multi-racialists was the publication in 1969 by Arthur Jensen in the *Harvard Educational Review*." With the appearance of sociobiology, the National Front claimed further vindication for its political stands: "Our racialist viewpoint, which sees the national family as an organic whole within which the individual fulfills his wider purpose of contributing to its strength and survival, is endorsed by the sociobiologists." At the time, the National Front was a rising force in England. Its strength was thought to have influenced politicians such as Margaret Thatcher, pressuring them to take strong anti-immigration stands.

A more intellectual and mainstream version of the National Front was prominent in France in the 1970s and 1980s. La Nouvelle Droite (The New Right) published its own journal, *Nouvelle Ecole* (*New School*), which promoted scientific racism and the superiority of the Nordic race. Despite these extreme views, the editor-in-chief, Alain de Benoist, received the grand prize from the Académie Française for his 1978 book *Vu de Droite* (*View from the Right*). Louis Pauwels, director general of the prestigious journal *Le Figaro*, was a strong supporter of *Nouvelle Ecole*. As a result, Pauwels regularly published columns by Alain de Benoist and other members of the Nouvelle Droite in *Le Figaro*. Like the National Front in England, La Nouvelle Droite had used the work of Arthur Jensen to support its racist and eugenic proposals. It now cited support from sociobiological theory:

> The laws of life make equality impossible. This is the revolutionary message of 300 of the greatest English and American scientists: the sociobiologists. (*Le Figaro*)

> Sociobiology is making spectacular progress, It cannot be ignored just because it is close to certain Nazi themes. (*Nouvelle Ecole*)

Wilson himself granted an interview to Le Figaro. In an article entitled "Confirmation: Intelligence Is Hereditary," he stated: "It has clearly been established that intelligence is, for the most part, inherited."

Such different but equally dramatic popular representations of sociobiology on the two sides of the Atlantic were exactly the consequences our group had worried about when we decided to submit the letter to the New York Review of Books. In the United States, at that time deeply divided over issues of women's rights, sociobiological arguments were being used by those who resisted changes in traditional sex roles. In England and France, where immigration was becoming an increasingly contentious issue, sociobiology's explanations for class structure and xenophobia were used to support the ideology of the growing extreme right-wing movements. The representations by Playboy on the one hand and Le Figaro on the other may have gone far beyond what Wilson and others had intended, but they were predictable consequences of using the prestige of science to give prescriptive advice to society. When Wilson, in his New Synthesis, presented speculations such as "if the planned society . . . were to deliberately steer its members past those stresses and conflicts that once gave the destructive phenotypes [aggression, dominance, violence] their Darwinian edge, the other phenotypes [cooperativeness, creativity, athletic zeal] might dwindle with them," he appeared to be offering a scientific rationale for conservative or even regressive social policies. The offer had not been ignored.

▲ ▲ ▲ The ongoing media coverage made clear that sociobiology was not a flash in the pan. The Sociobiology Study Group continued to write and speak publicly, conveying our criticisms of the science and its social uses. Because of our strong response, sociobiology, which had started out as a "revolutionary" new science on the front page of the *New York Times,* now began to be referred to as a "controversial" science. Debates, symposia, and books presented contrasting views of the scientific merits of this new science. If nothing else, we had raised questions in the public's mind about whether sociobiology was universally accepted in the scientific community.

Perhaps the most dramatic moment in the "sociobiology debate" and for our group the nadir of the controversy took place in February 1978, when the American Association for the Advancement of Science scheduled a symposium on sociobiology. A panel, including E. O. Wilson and Stephen Jay Gould, argued the science of sociobiology and its implications. During Wilson's talk, a group of young people walked up on the stage and poured water on Wilson's head, chanting, "E. O. Wilson you can't hide, we charge you with genocide." The Committee against Racism, which had organized the action, was affiliated with the Progressive Labor Party, the Maoist organization that years before I had discussed with Hilary Putnam. The members of the Sociobiology Study Group who were in the audience were dismayed by this action. First, we opposed the tactics of physical assault. Second, the accusations of genocide were ludicrous and incomprehensible, cheapened the word "genocide," and made the critics look ridiculous. I stood up from the audience after the incident and strongly denounced this action on behalf of Science for the People, making it clear that we opposed such behavior. Nevertheless, for years after and even today, the "water-pouring incident" has been attributed to Science for the People.

The Sociobiology Study Group would stay together for eleven years; the flood of popular interpretations of sociobiology continued unabated for nearly that long. To gauge the impact of pop sociobiology, we continued to survey popular magazines, school texts, and the news-oriented science journals. We held educational forums on Boston-area campuses and elsewhere and presented workshops and talks at annual meetings of the American Association for the Advancement of Science and the National Association of Biology Teachers. We not only spoke on sociobiology, but also organized a discussion on the biology of sex roles and another on genetics, race and IQ. In 1977, Barbara and I led a workshop on sociobiology for the Boston-Cambridge Ministry in Higher Education, an organization of campus ministries.

In 1983, the publication of a book by the anthropologist Derek Freeman "unmasking" the work of Margaret Mead launched a new phase in the sociobiology debate. Mead's anthropological studies of sexual behavior in Samoan tribes appeared to contradict sociobiologists' proposed universals of human nature. Her claims that attitudes toward sex, rape, and hierarchy differed dramatically depending on the social context became a new touchstone for the sociobiology debate. Freeman deemed Mead's work biased and invalid. The Sociobiology Study Group entered the fray, organizing a forum of anthropologists who commented on the status of Mead's work and on the significance of the controversy. Remarkably, a comparable sociobiology-related public storm arose in the year 2000 when the journalist Patrick Tierney, in his book, *Darkness at El Dorado*, attacked the work of the anthropologist Napoleon Chagnon. Tierney argued that Chagnon had exaggerated or even fomented the violent behavior of the Yanomamo Indians of Brazil that he recorded in his book. The Mead and Chagnon controversies were nearly perfect mirror images. As critics of sociobiology had cited Mead's work in support of their position, sociobiologists referred to Chagnon's *Yanomamo: The Fierce People* as prima facie evidence for their theories of human nature. The two anthropologists became icons for the two sides of the sociobiology debate. The critics of sociobiology came to the defense of Mead in the 1980s; the sociobiologists and evolutionary psychologists joined to attack Tierney's book in 2000.

The long life of the sociobiology controversy prompted the Sociobiology Study Group to prepare materials that brought together many of the issues in human behavioral genetics. We wrote some pieces for popular and academic journals, and we also published our own collection of articles, entitled *Biology as Destiny: Scientific Fact or Social Bias?* In 1984, we produced a slide show for high school classrooms, *Fate or Fiction: Biological Theories of Human Behavior.* Covering a range of behavioral genetics issues, the show was designed to give students a critical perspective on scientific conclusions about the role of genes in human behavior. We organized a retrospective on the sociobiology controversy in 1984, with talks by Dick Lewontin and Steve Gould, at the same time "premiering" our slide show. I still get requests for the show today from high school teachers.

The group lasted as long as it did, in part, because it fulfilled a personal need for many of us. Although its composition changed over time, the group always consisted of a vital and diverse mix of people from different disciplines. For those of us who worked in the natural sciences, this mix helped connect our science and the world into which it was being introduced. We learned from each other. In addition to our readings in biology, we discussed articles and books in anthropology, philosophy, and psychology. I found out perhaps more than I needed to know about different kinds of baboon societies, about kinship structures in far-off places such as the South Pacific and South Africa, about feminist psychoanalytic theory.

One of the most influential readings for me was a book by the primatologist Sarah Blaffer Hrdy. Hrdy, a firm believer in the sociobiological approach to understanding human societies, had worked with DeVore and Wilson at Harvard. But in *The Woman That Never Evolved*, published in 1981, Hrdy challenged the traditional view of male-female differences in primate societies. She showed how primatologists, almost entirely male, had ignored the behavior of females in their studies, concentrating on male dominance, aggression, and sexuality. Hrdy contrasted these studies with the work of a number of others in the field, mostly female, who had found as many instances of aggression, sexuality, "promiscuity," and dominance hierarchies among female primates as the male anthropologists had found among male primates. Hrdy explained that these different observations were sometimes due to which species of monkey the researchers chose to study. But, more strikingly, she showed that male researchers had either missed or failed to report many of the types of female primate behaviors that other researchers later found in the same species.

This book had three important consequences for the ongoing sociobiology debate. For some "pop sociobiologists," Hrdy's comprehensive survey of primatological studies forced a reexamination of important aspects of sociobiological arguments. Her analysis also could be taken as support for one of my group's strongest criticisms—that much of the theorizing on human behavior was based on a selective choice of data reflecting the biases of the theory constructor. Finally, Hrdy used the new information to build a different view of human female behavior, albeit one still based on sociobiological principles. Now there were (at least) two competing theories. How readily the conclusions of sociobiology and the resultant views of human social relationships could change simply by the choice of which species and which data fit best with certain social preconceptions! How could a science of human behavior that was so easily affected by the personal outlook of the researcher be taken as seriously as it was? One could look on the existence of these two competing accounts of female behavior as raising questions about the overall approach of "pop sociobiology." The two theories seemed to cancel each other out.

As the public exploitation of sociobiological themes, perhaps bereft of new angles, began to wane, a new incarnation appeared in the 1990s. The new field of "evolutionary psychology" includes as its spokespeople the British evolutionist Richard Dawkins, author of *The Selfish Gene*, the MIT linguist Steven Pinker, the Tufts University philosopher Daniel Dennett, and Robert Wright, the former editor of the *New Republic*. While citing theoretical advances in sociobiology in support of their theories, the evolutionary psychologists have been more restrained than their "pop sociobiology" predecessors in offering prescriptive advice to society.

▲ ▲ ▲ History has witnessed and will continue to witness repeated attempts to develop a genetic or evolutionary framework for explaining human social arrangements. Whatever the name given to the field, there remains the inescapable complication that the theories are constructed by scientists who are themselves social human beings trying to explain the social behavior of human beings. Researchers inevitably bring with them a set of personal assumptions that color the direction of their research, their interpretation of the data, and their conclusions. The very definition of human social traits and behaviors, such as intelligence, altruism, and criminality, varies according to the social or political perspective of the definer. Because of these social influences, we can look back at a century-long history of failed studies on the genetic basis of such traits and the ultimate rejection of over-arching theories that explain human social arrangements. It may be that we are reaching a point of scientific sophistication where behavioral genetic studies will begin to meet with more success. Nevertheless, the lesson taught by this history is that scientists in these fields should become much more sensitive to the tentativeness that should attend reports of such studies in light of their problematic nature. They should be aware of the social harm that can result from the premature proclamation of claims that are weakly founded. In most areas of science, we do not ask researchers to tone down their speculations. But scientists must be particularly careful when their science deals with questions of human import. They have entered the political arena.

▲ ▲ ▲ Of course, some scientists believe so firmly in their conclusions and in the social implications of their work that they eagerly go before the public and offer prescriptive advice. If their belief is that firm, that is absolutely their right and even their responsibility. For example, those of us who believe that the dangerous spread of antibiotic resistance is due to the overuse of antibiotics have an obligation to speak out to prevent potential disaster. By the same token, geneticists who believe that sociobiologists (or evolutionary psychologists) are making scientifically incorrect claims with potentially dangerous social consequences have the obligation to try to publicly correct those claims. It was this feeling of obligation that, among other factors, kept the Sociobiology Study Group together for so many years.

I'm Not Very Scary Anymore

"This section of the highway is maintained by Scary Larry." The curious sign appeared as Barbara and I drove through a violent sandstorm on our way to the Cliffhangers' Lodge. We had tried to set up camp at the base of the Vermillion Cliffs, a remote spot in northern Arizona. We planned to hike up the cliffs in the morning to find Indian rock art we had read about. But the billows of sand barreling off the desert floor forced us to seek shelter elsewhere.

We had no problem getting a room in the Lodge; the Vermillion Cliffs are not a popular tourist area. Safely ensconced in the Lodge's restaurant, we watched through the window as the sand swirled hypnotically, interposing a blinding barrier between us and the outside world. Then, like an apparition emerging from the clouds of sand, a grizzled old man materialized. He began to pace up and down on the outside porch. "Who's that guy?" we asked the waiter. "Oh, that's Scary Larry. He's lived around here for years."

As we walked along the porch to our room after dinner, we saw the pacer heading toward us. "Are you Scary Larry?" Barbara asked. "Yes," he replied, "but, I'm not very scary anymore."

▲ ▲ ▲ Scary Larry's self-reflective comment struck a chord with me. I reflected on how much the outside world's image of me as an

Figure 4. My 1980 photograph in *Smithsonian* (above) and my second *Smithsonian* portrait in 1990 (right).

activist in science had changed over the years. Two photographs of me in *Smithsonian* magazine, published ten years apart, symbolized this apparent transformation. The "before-and-after" pictures showed the metamorphosis of a menace in the scientific community into a saint. I was no longer "very scary." (And Larry really wasn't either. The day after our meeting, "Friendly Larry" helped us find a route up the cliffs to our rock art.)

The first picture appeared in a 1980 *Smithsonian* article on the sociobiology debate written by Albert Rosenfeld. Rosenfeld laid out in stark terms the scientific and political conflict over sociobiology. Two Harvard professors, E. O. Wilson, "his name . . . now synonymous with sociobiology," and Jon Beckwith, critic of pop sociobiology and "ultimate arch-radical," represented the two sides of the debate. By choosing me as the foil to Wilson, Rosenfeld

Copyright Peter Menzel/www.menzelphoto.com

managed to ignore the substantive scientific issues. Instead, he constructed a dichotomy between those who wanted to see science progress and those who wanted to hold it back. According to Rosenfeld, I was among the "anti-geneticist[s]" who asked, "Do we really want to know?" while those wiser scientists on the other side, like Wilson, looked upon new knowledge "with exhilaration." It seemed as if I had an image problem. Perhaps this extreme characterization stemmed from my involvement in a series of controversies beginning in 1969—the press conference, the donation of the Lilly prize to the Black Panthers, my activism in Science for the People, the bitter XYY episode, and now the challenge to sociobiology.

But the characterization of the sociobiology "dichotomy" was false. The critiques by the Sociobiology Study Group had never included calls for an end to sociobiological research. We responded to the uncritical media response, pointing out the scientific failings of the pop sociobiological program and its misrepresentation of genetic knowledge to support social prescriptions. Nevertheless, this unaccustomed critique by one group of scientists of the validity of the work of another group, couched partly in political terms, had elicited a fearful response from many within the scientific community. As in the XYY controversy, some, like Rosenfeld, seemed reflexively to take this criticism as an attempt to halt scientific research. Perhaps my earlier opposition to recombinant DNA research influenced this interpretation. This simplification of the terms of the sociobiology debate as a struggle between defenders versus would-be destroyers of science—heroes versus villains— thus became the theme of the *Smithsonian* article.

The photographs illustrating the Rosenfeld article highlighted the author's depiction of right and wrong. *Smithsonian's* photographer posed E. O. Wilson in his lab, dressed in tie and tweedy jacket, examining his ant colonies, looking like the archetypal Harvard professor. On his visit to my lab, the same photographer suggested that I put on my windbreaker and day-pack to pose for some outdoor pictures. In front of the Harvard Medical School buildings, he took a series of exposures using a fish-eye lens. The published photograph portrayed a somber and humorless man, dressed more like a street demonstrator than an academic, with his nose, enhanced by the fish-eye lens, nearly dominating the picture. A backdrop of gray skies and the austere Harvard Medical School buildings added a menacing quality to the photograph. The pictorial message: Which of these men would you trust—the well-dressed, respectable professor or the "arch-radical"?

Ten years later, in 1990, E. O. Wilson was still publicly prominent, but now receiving more attention for his efforts to save the world's disappearing species of plants and animals than for sociobiology. And I, the "arch-radical," had just been appointed to a U.S.

government working group asked to deal with the "ethical, legal, and social implications" (ELSI) associated with the Human Genome Project. *Smithsonian* magazine commissioned Stephen Hall, a science writer, to prepare an article on the Human Genome Project. As in 1980, I was interviewed by the author of this article and again posed for photographs. This time the photographer (not the same one) stationed me at various sites in my laboratory. I didn't notice that the backdrop for one of these poses was the round disk of a roller drum used for growing tubes of bacteria. When the photograph appeared in *Smithsonian*, it was obvious that the disk was meant to appear as a halo behind my head. ("Just move your head a little bit more to the right.") In the years since the article appeared, friends have kidded me about that photo—"you don't really seem to be a saint." An unknown "admirer" sent me a pasted-together composition in which my head replaced that of a real saint from a medieval work of art.

In Hall's article, I was not the scary arch-radical anymore. I had been transformed into someone who was on the "side of the angels" (or at least the saints). As when Xandra Breakefield called me for ethical advice, I puzzled over how this transmutation from "bad guy" to "good guy" had taken place and why. Had I changed? Had the environment within science changed?

The earlier *Smithsonian* article appeared toward the end of a period of political activism among scientists, a movement driven by the social upheavals of the 1960s and early 1970s. A rule of the culture of science until then had been that scientists didn't contaminate themselves with public contact. Once the Vietnam War had politicized American society, it became more acceptable to be a scientist and an activist. Political activism eventually led some of us scientists to question the assumptions that influenced science itself. We challenged the myth that science is a neutral pursuit, uncontaminated by social and political concerns. When our activism entered the realm of science through such groups as Science for the People, many of our fellow scientists reacted negatively.

Continuing demonstrations against the Vietnam War and the growing radicalization of university campuses sparked a resurgence of interest in Marx's vision of class struggle. Opponents in any controversy were practically class enemies. It went both ways. In extreme instances, someone like E. O. Wilson was seen as a conscious agent of ruling-class interests and someone like myself was depicted as a Marxist revolutionary (despite the fact that I had never read Marx). Neither portrait reflected reality.

Those of us who publicly raised concerns about the social consequences of science were mistrusted by other scientists. Scientist-activists were dismissed with suggestions that their research had gone down hill. David Suzuki, a brilliant Canadian *Drosophila* (fruit fly) geneticist, is a case in point. In the 1970s, Suzuki spent less and less time on genetic research at the University of British Columbia and more and more time as a media figure presenting science to the public. His television programs frequently integrated social issues into discussions of scientific subjects. In his autobiography, Suzuki talks of the reaction among his colleagues: "My growing involvement in television was resented by my fellow professors . . . I heard [reasons]: I was on an ego trip, my science wasn't good enough so I shifted areas, I was wasting my time." Similarly, people like Jim Watson used the labels "kooks" or "second-rate scientists" to describe scientists who expressed concerns about the hazards of recombinant DNA research in the 1970s. Although Watson had been one of the initiators of the moratorium on such research, he became dismayed at the strong public reaction against this new technology that followed.

In much the same way, Benno Müller-Hill experienced hostility from the German scientific community after the publication of his book *Murderous Science*, about the deep involvement of the German scientific establishment in Nazi eugenics and human experimentation. Müller-Hill has written of his experiences giving lectures at German universities on the history of human genetics under National Socialism. At the end of one speech, scientists in the audience subjected him to personal attacks—"What are your real motives?" "You weren't there; only one who was there has the right to talk." Ironically, members of the German Green Party also attacked Müller-Hill after his talk at one of their conventions. The Greens had invited him to speak on the assumption that his courageous exposés of the role of German geneticists in the Nazi era indicated a more general opposition to genetic research. Müller-Hill's overall support of contemporary developments in genetics was anathema to the Greens. You're either for us or you're against us.

By 1990, the cooling down of the activism and rhetoric of the 1960s had modified the sense of them versus us. In the absence of that rhetoric, the old antagonisms faded. When geneticists, many of them involved in biotechnology companies, were regularly calling press conferences to announce their discoveries, it was hard to continue disparaging scientists who went public with their concerns about science. At the same time, some aspects of the critiques of science had infiltrated mainstream thinking about science. It had become accepted wisdom that scientists should at least pay lip service to the concept of social responsibility. Even as early as 1973, a group of prominent biologists (including Jim Watson) had called for caution in the implementation of recombinant DNA research. They proposed a temporary moratorium on those genetic studies while the potential consequences of the research were explored. In the 1970s and 1980s, the annual meetings of the American Association for the Advancement of Science featured more and more sessions on controversial social implications of science. And then, in 1989, Jim Watson, newly appointed director of the government's Human Genome Project, announced that he would establish a program to explore and anticipate the ethical, legal, and social implications of the project. It was to a committee charged with setting up this program that I was appointed in that same year.

The origins of the Human Genome Project go back to the early 1970s, when the development of recombinant DNA technology and methods for sequencing DNA ushered in a revolution in molecular biology. By the mid-1980s, a decade of rapid progress had opened up hitherto unimagined vistas for the future of biology. Geneticists were locating a host of genes associated with human diseases such as Huntington's disease, muscular dystrophy, and breast cancer. In 1985, Robert Sinsheimer, a bacterial geneticist and chancellor of the University of California at Santa Cruz, proposed the idea of a "human genome project." The term human genome referred to the collection of chromosomes that each of our cells contain. The "project" should concentrate the attention of the genetics community on a coordinated effort to determine the complete DNA sequence of all of these chromosomes. Such an achievement would provide the sequence of every gene that human cells contain. Finding genes for every human genetic disease would be much easier and faster if the complete map and sequence of all human chromosomes were available. This information should also make possible a deeper understanding of the normal development and functioning of the human body and of the diseases that affect those processes. Sinsheimer's proposal was taken most seriously by Charles DeLisi, a physicist at the Department of Energy, who proposed that the DOE head the project. Some leading biologists, concerned that DeLisi's proposal would lead to a shift in funding from the National Institutes of Health to the DOE, urged that the NIH become involved in the project.

Biologists debated the scientific merits of the human genome during the late 1980s. Many argued that such a mega-project would divert resources from smaller and potentially more valuable basic science research efforts. Others warned of the dangerous social and ethical consequences that could attend such a project. They worried that the ability to characterize people by their genome sequences would lead to a vast interference in people's lives. Nevertheless, the grand-sounding nature of the project captured the imagination of the public and the politicians. Some proponents compared sequencing the human genome to previous focused scientific efforts such as "putting a man on the moon" or the Manhattan Project. Given its political attractiveness and the scientific stature of its leading supporters, the project was soon funded by Congress. In 1989, the Human Genome Project began as a joint effort between the NIH and the DOE, with Jim Watson as its first director. Watson immediately announced that he would set aside 3–5 percent of the project's budget for the ELSI program. The ELSI program was unprecedented; never before had the initiation of a scientific project been accompanied by an investigation of its potential social consequences. The two to three million dollars available for ELSI issues represented the largest funding ever from either private or public sources for the investigation of ethical and social issues related to scientific research.

▲ ▲ ▲ My appointment to the ELSI committee can be traced back to changes that took place in the Sociobiology Study Group. Just at the time that discussions about the possibility of the Human Genome Project were beginning, the Sociobiology Study Group was questioning whether we should continue devoting our energies to the sociobiology issue. Media interest in sociobiological explanations of human behavior had largely disappeared by the mid-1980s, even though the scientific field itself had established a significant foothold in academia. Increasingly, we lost our motivation to confront sociobiological ideas as they faded from prominence in the public arena. The potentially dangerous public impact of science was our incentive to action. When such science retreated into its academic setting, we were no longer impelled to confront it.

Yet, as a group, we wanted to continue working together. We shared a commitment to exploring the social consequences of scientific progress and to doing it not alone, but collectively. We had developed close working and personal relationships. Members of the group had collaborated in the writing of papers. I had a particularly close writing relationship with Joseph Alper, a chemist from the University of Massachusetts. Our joint writing efforts have continued to this day. But what would be the focus of the group if we were to continue? In this same period, still years before the inception of the Human Genome Project, human genetics was progressing at a remarkable pace. Even as we continued to explore the social impact of sociobiology, we had also begun to follow developments in the new human genetics. Our interest flowed naturally out of the prior involvement of many of us in issues such as the genetics-race-IQ and XYY male controversies. Early in 1986, we devoted several meetings to discussions about the future of the Sociobiology Study Group. It seemed an easy decision to change directions and begin to examine the social implications of the new human genetics. We renamed ourselves the Genetic Screening Study Group.

One general problem stood out as a major potential consequence of advances in human genetics. The dramatic progress in this field would make possible the collection of enormous amounts of genetic information about individuals, families, and even different ethnic groups. The Human Genome Project would greatly enhance this capability. How would society confront and use this information? Given the past problems with misuse and misrepresentation of genetic findings, the need to establish safeguards seemed obvious. We invited to one of our meetings Philip Reilly, a lawyer who was interested in ethical issues in genetics. Phil, who had come to a few Science for the People meetings many years earlier, had since then published the major work on genetic screening and the law. He had recently received his medical degree and then been chosen to head the Eunice Kennedy Shriver Center for Mental Retardation in Waltham, Massachusetts.

We asked Phil whether there was any evidence that people had suffered negative consequences as a result of the availability of genetic information about them. We knew of isolated incidents—the problems associated with XYY screening, the use of sickle cell testing to reject applicants for health insurance and employment. Were these only isolated incidents? Phil told us that no one had ever asked this question. For example, he knew of no surveys that had looked for cases of discrimination by surveying people who had undergone genetic tests. He also pointed out that there were no laws to protect people against such discrimination. It seemed obvious that employers and insurance companies could have a strong interest in new ways of predicting who would remain healthy and who would get sick. We wanted to know if people who were perfectly healthy, but had received genetic test results indicating susceptibility to a particular disease, suffered any discrimination, such as losing insurance or a job. But without any evidence or examples, "genetic discrimination," as we called it, remained a theoretical problem. Before we could discuss public policy on genetic discrimination, we had to know whether it existed. We would make our own attempt to gather data on this subject.

One of our members, Paul Billings, a medical genetic researcher and clinician, suggested that genetic counselors and clinical geneticists might have encountered examples of genetic discrimination with their patients. Genetic disease support groups might also be a source of such information. These organizations, each of which had formed to improve the lives of those suffering from a specific genetic disease, were made up of members who suffered from the disease and the families of those with the condition. These groups actively promoted research on the disease and the development of treatments and cures. Paul placed an ad in genetics journals. We asked for reports of instances where people who were not symptomatic for a disease had received positive genetic test results and, as a result, had been discriminated against. We also asked other geneticists we knew in the Boston are about such cases and contacted a few of the genetic disease support groups. Although we had no grant support to pay for this small survey, we were still able to identify a number of likely cases. We followed up the individual cases with personal contacts and did our best to verify instances of discrimination. We discussed the cases at our group meetings to pick out those that fit our definition of genetic discrimination.

A pattern emerged. Most of the people who believed they had suffered genetic discrimination had been unable to obtain health insurance or had encountered employment problems. Although people did report genetic discrimination in other settings, these two areas represented the majority of the cases. We now foresaw that as the number of genetic tests increased, particularly with the impetus of the Human Genome Project, the prospects for discrimination could increase enormously. In fact, one could argue that since everyone carries some genes that make him or her susceptible to one condition or another, everyone could be a potential victim of genetic discrimination. We prepared a report on the survey and submitted it to the *American Journal of Human Genetics*, the leading journal in the field of human genetics. It was accepted and published in April 1992.

This study and publication represented a different mode of action for many of us. While those of us in the Genetic Screening Study Group who were scientists published our own laboratory research in mainstream journals, much of our writing on the social implications of genetics had appeared in journals such as *Science* for the *People* magazine, with its circulation of four thousand, or in other left-wing publications. We had not imagined presenting our social critiques to large-circulation journals. We didn't realize that the environment had changed and that many of the things we had been saying for years were now more widely accepted. We no longer had to write as outsiders—we could reach a wider audience. It took some of the younger members of the group to set us straight. Eric Lander, who was then a mathematician moving into genetics, joined the group after taking my genetics course at the Harvard Medical School. He and Paul Billings convinced us that we weren't quite so scary any more.

The impact of our *American Journal of Human Genetics* paper was impressive. Newspapers and magazines picked up on "genetic discrimination," sometimes discovering dramatic cases themselves. On the basis of this first report, we obtained a grant from the DOE's ELSI wing of the Human Genome Project to do a more systematic survey of genetic disease support groups. A second paper covering this study appeared in the journal *Science and Engineering Ethics*. Other groups launched surveys on genetic discrimination. Even though there was considerable debate over just how widespread such discrimination was, the public discussion of the issue of genetic discrimination led to the passage of bills outlawing the practice in a large number of states.

During this period of transition for the group, we had a second interest: science journalism. We had watched the astounding press coverage of sociobiology and the comparable hype surrounding the establishment of the Human Genome Project. We had seen how historically, and still today, weak or even fraudulent science had attracted far more media attention than it deserved. Problems existed both in the way scientific information was presented by scientists and in the way it was publicized by the news-oriented science journals such as *Science* and *Nature*. The stature of science and the imprimatur of prestigious scientific journals led the media to present scientific reports uncritically. On the journalistic side, pressure from editors to make scientific stories sound as newsworthy and broadly appealing as, for example, political scandals led to further exaggerations of these reports. As I have described elsewhere in this book, this sequence from the lab to scientific journals to the media often had a social impact far exceeding the merits of the original science.

We decided to organize forums where scientists and journalists could participate in give-and-take on the communication of science to the public. Science is usually not the hard and fast truth that is presented to journalists. Scientists like others have their agendas and their biases. When a dramatic new drug or treatment is proclaimed, what if the scientist reporting it has connections to a biotechnology company that profits from the announcement? When a geneticist announces a gene for intelligence, what social assumptions might be incorporated into the study of this murky area? How do such influences affect the validity of the scientific claims? Such questions should lead to deeper probing by reporters into the scientific quality of the research findings. Furthermore, science is filled with controversies, many of which are unknown to journalists. Conversely, scientists have little understanding of the science journalists' agendas and they do not know what pressures and constraints editors place on journalists. For instance, one of the main complaints I hear from scientists about science journalists is the nature of the headlines that appear over the stories the journalists write. Practically none of these scientists realize that headlines for articles are written by headline writers, not by the journalists.

Between 1986 and 1994, we organized four conferences under the rubric "Science and Journalism." At each of these, we brought together 200–300 scientists, science journalists, teachers, and science students to discuss the problems of communicating science to the public. The four conferences were titled "Covering Controversy in Science" (1986), "Are We Ready for the New Genetic Medicine?" (1989), "Genes and Human Behavior: A New Era?" (1991), and "Genes That Make News, News That Makes Genes" (1994). Each consisted of keynote addresses and a series of panels. A panel would usually include two scientists who held opposing views on a scientific issue, a journalist who had covered the issue, and a speaker representing the public. For example, one of the panels at the 1994 conference began with talks by Dr. Fred Li, a cancer genetics researcher and Dr. Neil Holtzman, a pediatric geneticist worried about the implications of testing for mutations that predispose to cancer. Laurie Garrett, a science writer for Newsday, followed with a talk about journalistic coverage of the "breast cancer gene." The session ended with a talk by Sandra Steingraber, author of a book on her own experiences with breast cancer, who expressed her concerns that the exaggerated publicity surrounding the new genetics had caused the media to downplay the environmental sources of cancer. Other panels with a similarly diverse composition dealt with reports of genetic loci associated with homosexuality and criminality.

It was our 1989 conference that led to my joining the ELSI Working Group of the Human Genome Project. We invited as a speaker Dr. Nancy Wexler, well known for her energetic role in promoting the successful search for the Huntington's disease gene. Huntington's is a debilitating neurological disorder that affects its victims in mid-life and results in progressive loss of memory, increasingly erratic behavior, increasing lack of control over bodily movements, and ultimately death. Early in the twentieth century, Charles Davenport, a leading spokesperson for the eugenics movement discussed earlier, had shown that Huntington's was a dominantly inherited condition. Woody Guthrie, perhaps the most famous folk singer in the United States, suffered and died from Huntington's.

The origins of Nancy's campaign to promote genetic studies on

Huntington's are movingly described in a book by her sister Alice Wexler, *Mapping Fate: A Memoir of Family, Risk, and Genetic Research.* Nancy and Alice learned in the early 1950s that their mother had been diagnosed with Huntington's. The diagnosis prompted Nancy and her father, Milton, to devote their energies to promoting research into the basis of this disease. Nancy, who had been trained as a clinical psychologist, began to study extended Huntington's families in the Lake Maracaibo region of Venezuela, where the disease was rampant, and her findings were to provide the key material necessary for the discovery of the Huntington's gene. Pinpointing the location of the chromosomal region associated with Huntington's was one of the great early successes of the new human genetics.

Alice Wexler in her book recounts the Wexler family history, their involvement in establishing the Huntington's Disease Collaborative Project, and, finally, the identification of the gene. Despite her exhilarating account of the progress toward mapping the gene, she finishes the book wondering what the benefits of this finding will be. The detection of the Huntington's gene helped raise and crystallize many of the social problems associated with genetic testing. The two sisters themselves questioned whether they wanted to be tested for the Huntington's mutation. Since there is no cure for the disease, they worried about the psychological impact of learning what was to come. Alice asks whether the medical system is prepared to counsel and advise people who choose to be tested. Will positive test information be kept private? Will it be used to discriminate in insurance and employment, as we had found in our surveys? What are the prospects for cures once a gene is found? To date, medical science has produced no cures for Huntington's or for any of the diseases for which genes have been found by the new genetic techniques. In most cases, the development of treatments or cures will take many years of work and some significant breakthroughs.

When Nancy Wexler spoke on a panel at our conference, she described the impact of Huntington's, a disorder that has behavioral consequences, on family and social life in the Venezuelan community she studied. As a member of the same panel, I spoke of the many examples where discoveries of genes for behavioral traits had been reported. I noted that the history of this field was replete with positive publications and then retractions or refutations. Yet the media repeatedly reported each new claim uncritically and rarely mentioned any subsequent withdrawal of claims. Especially in the genetics of mental illness and human social behaviors and aptitudes, the media had a long record of enthusiastic and dramatic coverage of scientific reports that turned out to be mistaken.

At the end of the conference, Nancy asked me if I would be willing to be part of a group that Jim Watson was forming within the Human Genome Project. Jim had appointed her chair of the Working Group on Ethical, Legal, and Social Implications of the Human Genome Project, whose mission was to anticipate any potential adverse social consequences of the project and to suggest means of preventing these consequences. Nancy had good reason to be aware of the loaded nature of genetic information. Her intimate knowledge of a genetic disease, her own dilemma about whether or not to be tested, and her vibrant personality must have made her seem an ideal choice for this position. Furthermore, she had the confidence of the genetics community because of her close ties with a number of researchers. Her credibility was important because many geneticists tended to scoff at nonscientists trained in ethics or other non-hard science fields who expressed concerns about genetics. I accepted Nancy's invitation. My appointment to the Working Group in 1989 resulted in the dramatically different second photograph of me in *Smithsonian*.

▲ ▲ ▲ There was one more picture to come in *Smithsonian*. In 1999, Barbara wrote an article about my close escape from death.

While hiking in southern Utah's White Canyon, we came to an expanse of water filling the canyon and blocking our way. I took off my clothes and started to walk through the water, to test out its depth. Chest-deep in water, I suddenly found myself being sucked down into the sand at the bottom. It wasn't just sand; it was quicksand. By some series of weird contortions (according to Barbara, who watched helplessly), I managed to free myself and scramble back to safety. No photographer was present this time. Barbara's article instead was accompanied by a cartoon of me, quite nude and scared (but not scary anymore).

CHAPTER 11

Story-Telling in Science

In 1958, François Jacob was sitting in a movie theater with his wife, Lise, when the explanation for gene regulation came to him. "And suddenly a flash," is the way he describes his mid-movie intuition that repressors must act directly on genes to inhibit their expression. Francis Crick's 1961 experiments that led to the demonstration of the triplet nature of the genetic code derived unexpectedly from his attempts to test a misconceived theory of protein synthesis. Crick had the idea that amino acid sequences of proteins are translated from RNA molecules that curve back on themselves—a mechanism he called the "loopy code" theory. But in the course of testing this "loopy" model, Crick and his colleagues performed some experiments that serendipitously illuminated how the genetic code actually works.

Jacob and Crick do not tell these stories in the journal articles where they first reported two of molecular biology's major milestones. We learn of the genesis of their contributions only long after the original publications—for instance, in Jacob's 1987 autobiography, *The Statue Within*, or in Horace Freeland Judson's *Eighth Day of Creation*, a history of molecular biology published in 1979. The seminal papers include none of the wrong turns or inspirational moments. The work is presented as though it were impeccably conceived and the conclusions were logically deduced. As the geneticist Robert Edgar aptly said, scientific publications are "fabrications, pieced together to create pleasing stories which, although they are sometimes reflections of nature, are rarely mirrors of the scientist at work."

I reflect on this "methodology" of scientific presentations, because of twists and turns in my own research that began in the late 1980s and that continue to this day. When my colleagues and I attempted to publish a paper that included the tortuous story of this work, we encountered resistance and disapproval on the part of scientific journals. The tale begins in 1970, when I was in Naples and starting to think about switching my research program from studying gene regulation to exploring protein secretion.

Proteins are the main functional components of all living organisms. Cells retain most of their proteins inside the cytoplasm, which makes up the bulk of the cell mass. But a smaller number of proteins are transferred out of the cytoplasm. Some proteins enter into membrane-enclosed compartments within the cell and others migrate from the cell into the surrounding milieu. Human hormones, such as insulin and human growth hormone as well as antibodies, are proteins secreted across our cells' cytoplasmic membranes into the bloodstream. Once in the bloodstream, these proteins are transported to places in the body where they are needed.

Bacteria also secrete a fraction of their proteins across their cytoplasmic membrane. However, in the case of *Escherichia coli*, which has a second membrane surrounding the cell, most of these secreted proteins end up in an aqueous compartment, called the periplasm, which lies between the two membranes. I was interested in how the cell is able to know that one protein should remain in the cytoplasm while another one should be secreted into the periplasm. It seemed that there must be information in the amino acid sequence of a secreted protein that acts as a signal to the cell, telling it that this is a protein that wants to get out. I hoped that learning something about secretion signals and their recognition in bacteria would also help explain how human cells secrete their important proteins.

I decided to approach the secretion problem by dissecting the gene for a secreted protein in order to determine what portion of the protein contained the amino acid sequence that corresponded to the "secretion signal." The method of dissection I hit upon was to fuse together portions of two genes, one coding for a periplasmic protein and one for a cytoplasmic protein. This gene fusion would express a fused protein composed of a portion of the periplasmic protein and a portion of the cytoplasmic protein. My fellow researchers and I would then ask whether the cytoplasmic protein could be exported across the membrane. If this worked, we could determine how much of the periplasmic protein had to be attached to the cytoplasmic protein in order for this export to take place. At this point, I combined my interest in protein secretion with our earlier experience in studying the β-galactosidase gene, lacZ. The two fit together nicely. β-galactosidase was a cytoplasmic protein and we had developed techniques for fusing the lacZ gene to other genes. We would fuse the gene for a secreted protein to the lacZ gene encoding β-galactosidase, and ask whether it was possible, in this way, to alter the location of β-galactosidase from the cytoplasm to the periplasm.

We now needed to choose which secreted protein we would use for these experiments. I first thought of the protein alkaline phosphatase, an enzyme located in the E. coli periplasm that helps the cell to find sources of phosphate for its growth. This choice was inspired by my close relationship with my colleague Luigi Gorini and his wife, Annamaria Torriani. Annamaria had worked with alkaline phosphatase for nearly her entire career, beginning with her stay in Jacques Monod's laboratory in the 1950s. Together, Annamaria and

I collaborated on initial studies in the mid-1970s. In 1976, a new postdoctoral fellow, Thomas Silhavy, arrived in my lab, bringing with him experience with some other secreted proteins. He suggested we also use, in our gene fusion experiments, two proteins that E. coli needed in order to digest the sugar maltose, the maltose binding protein and the maltoporin. Tom had worked for a brief time at the Institut Pasteur in Paris with my friend Maxime Schwartz, an expert on the proteins of E. coli involved in maltose metabolism. (Maxime and I were jokingly referred to by other scientists as the Lac Panther and the Maltose Falcon because of our friendship and after my donation to the Black Panthers.)

It was while initiating these genetic experiments that my colleagues and I read of important and relevant findings in the field of protein secretion from another laboratory. Gunter Blobel and Bernhard Dobberstein, working at Rockefeller University in New York City were studying the secretion of proteins by animal cells. They had found that all secreted proteins examined contained a sequence of amino acids at the very beginning of the protein (the amino-terminus) that was removed from the proteins after they had crossed cellular membranes. They proposed that this "signal sequence" was required for protein secretion and presented a hypothesis that explained many features of the secretion process. There was now concrete evidence for the existence of signals for secretion in animal cells. Perhaps, we thought, the mechanism for this process would be the same in bacterial cells.

We readily constructed gene fusions that coded for hybrid proteins in which β-galactosidase was attached to the end (carboxy-terminus) of each of the three secreted proteins, alkaline phosphatase, maltoporin, and the maltose binding protein. When we then asked what happens to the β-galactosidase of the hybrid proteins, we were surprised by the answer. We had expected one of two possible consequences: either the β-galactosidase attached to the secreted protein would follow the secreted protein into the periplasm, or the β-galactosidase would ignore any signals present in the secreted protein and remain in its original location, the cytoplasm. Instead, we found that while the normally secreted portion of the fused protein was transferred across the membrane into the periplasm as usual, the β-galactosidase portion was unable to follow it. Instead, on its way to the periplasm, it became stuck in the cytoplasmic membrane. It was neither in the cytoplasm nor in the periplasm. Embedded in this unaccustomed membrane location, the β-galactosidase was distorted in its structure and, as a result, completely lacked its normal ability to break down the sugar lactose for E. coli growth.

These results were, at first, a great disappointment to us. Could we draw any conclusions about the location of signals in the secreted protein from such half-way results? But our disappointment soon turned to excitement when Tom Silhavy realized that the properties of the bacteria producing the hybrid protein might prove to be a powerful tool for doing genetic studies on the secretion signal of proteins. He pointed out that it must be the signal in the secreted protein that was directing β-galactosidase to the membrane where the enzyme got stuck, thus causing it to lose its activity and causing the cells to lose their ability to break down lactose. If this was true, anything that interfered with the signal and stopped it from bringing the β-galactosidase to the membrane would restore the normal cytoplasmic location of the enzyme and allow the cells to use lactose again. The most obvious way in which interference with the signal might be achieved would be by mutations in the portion of the fused gene that encoded the signal portion of the secreted protein. Mutations that prevented the signal sequence of the secreted protein from working properly should restore β-galactosidase activity. Without an effective signal sequence, cells could no longer recognize the hybrid proteins as proteins that should be secreted; the entire protein would remain in the cytoplasm. (See Figure 5.)

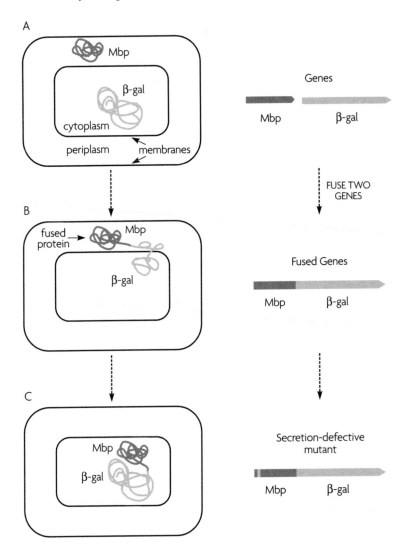

Tom reasoned that if we looked for mutants of strains producing these fusions that grew on lactose, we would obtain mutations that inactivated the signal portion of the secreted protein. Analysis of these mutations should allow us to determine the location of the mutations in the gene and, consequently, the place and nature of the secretion signal in the exported protein. Tom, by this time an assistant professor, along with his student Scott Emr, selected for mutants in which maltoporin could no longer guide β-galactosidase into the membrane and the cells would now grow on lactose. The mutations they found had changed the very beginning (the amino-terminus) of the maltoporin protein. (Even here, I have had to smooth out the story. The actual procedure Scott and Tom used to obtain these mutants is a little more complex than I have described. To make it easy to follow I have left out another property of the fusion strains that facilitated this genetic approach.)

Phillip Bassford, a postdoctoral fellow in my lab, and Susan Michaelis, a graduate student, used gene fusions to obtain signal sequence mutations in the genes for the two other secreted pro-

---

Figure 5 *(facing page).* Using gene fusions to obtain mutations affecting protein secretion. In contrast to Figure 1 (on page 30), this figure shows the bacteria with both of its two membranes and the periplasmic space that lies between them. A: Ordinarily, the bacteria express the two proteins Mbp (maltose binding protein) and β-gal (β-galactosidase) as separate proteins from separate genes. Mbp is in the periplasm and β-gal in the cytoplasm. B: Using genetic techniques, my colleagues and I fuse the two genes together so that the fused gene codes for one long single protein instead of the two previously separate proteins. This Mbp–β-gal hybrid protein is partly transferred to the periplasm and partly remains in the cytoplasm. The β-gal is inactivated and the cells cannot grow on lactose as a source of carbon. C. We select for mutants of the bacterial strain that can grow on lactose again. Some of these have mutations in the signal sequence of Mbp that prevent the attempted export of the hybrid protein to the periplasm. It remains in the cytoplasm, where the β-galactosidase again becomes active.

teins, maltose binding protein (Figure 5) and alkaline phosphatase. Again, we found that the mutations had altered the amino-terminal region of the proteins. In all three cases, we took the mutations from the gene fusions and introduced them into the genes coding for the original secreted proteins. All the intact proteins, maltose binding protein, maltoporin, and alkaline phosphatase, now contained amino acid changes in their signal sequences. The normally secreted proteins no longer crossed the cytoplasmic membrane into the periplasm. They remained in the cytoplasm. Tom's and our experiments had shown that these signals were essential for the cell to be able to recognize these proteins as ones to be secreted. We had obtained convincing genetic evidence for the signal hypothesis of protein export proposed by Gunter Blobel and Bernhard Dobberstein.

These initial genetic studies on protein secretion generated two very different projects in my laboratory. First, in 1983, Susan Michaelis pursued studies with strains that contained the signal sequence alterations in alkaline phosphatase. Ordinarily, when this protein is secreted into the periplasm, it exhibits an enzymatic activity that cleaves chemical bonds formed between phosphate ions and other molecules—hence the name phosphatase. However, when the alkaline phosphatase protein carried a defective signal sequence and was thus mislocalized to the cytoplasm, it lost its enzymatic activity.

Why was alkaline phosphatase active as an enzyme in one compartment of the cell, the periplasm, but inactive in another, the cytoplasm? We came up with a reasonable explanation. Alkaline phosphatase, in order to assemble into an active enzyme, must form certain chemical bonds between amino acids located far from one another within its protein sequence. Specifically, each of two pairs of the sulfurous amino acid cysteine join together by what are called disulfide bonds. The two disulfide bonds in alkaline phosphatase confer stability on the protein, preventing it from falling apart. We theorized that the disulfide bonds necessary for alkaline phosphatase activity could not form when the protein was in the cytoplasm. There were reasons to think that the periplasm was chemically a more favorable environment than the cytoplasm for the formation of such bonds. The difference in environments between the two compartments could explain why alkaline phosphatase was inactive in the cytoplasm. Alan Derman, one of my graduate students, then showed that our theory was correct. Alkaline phosphatase expressed in the periplasm contained disulfide bonds; when the same protein was expressed in the cytoplasm it had no disulfide bonds.

These findings raised two new questions in my mind: What are the specific factors in the cytoplasm that prevent formation of disulfide bonds and what are those in the periplasm that promote formation of disulfide bonds? It took almost seven years, and an unexpected result, for us to come upon the explanation for the difference in the presence of protein disulfide bonds in the two cellular compartments. This accidental discovery arose out of our continued efforts to understand protein secretion.

While some of my group began to pursue studies on disulfide bonds, a new postdoctoral fellow, Donald Oliver, took up the protein secretion project. We now knew that the cells are able to recognize signal sequences at the beginning of proteins as signals for secretion. But how these sequences worked was a complete mystery. That a signal sequence, on its own, would be sufficient to cause a protein to cross a membrane seemed unlikely. The hydrophobic (water-aversive) nature of the membrane still seemed like a formidable barrier to the penetration of hydrophilic (water-seeking) proteins. There must be cellular components, a "secretion machinery," that recognized signal sequences and helped proteins to traverse the membrane. Scott Emr and Tom Silhavy had obtained evidence for one such component.

We knew that mutations altering signal sequences made secreted proteins unrecognizable by the presumed secretion machinery. If that secretion machinery really existed, then it also should be possible to find the complementary type of mutations, those that altered components of the machinery so that they were no longer able to recognize signal sequences. In strains carrying such mutations, proteins with normal signal sequences could no longer be distinguished by the cell as proteins to be secreted. We predicted that such mutations, just like signal sequence mutations, would prevent β-galactosidase fused to a secreted protein from being incorporated into the cell membrane, resulting in the cytoplasmic location of β-galactosidase. The cells would be able to digest lactose again. This property would allow us to obtain mutants that would help us identify the components of our proposed "machinery."

We repeated the genetic selection for growth on lactose with an E. coli strain expressing the maltose binding protein–β-galactosidase fusion. But this time, we looked for mutations not in the gene fusion itself but rather in other genes on the bacterial chromosome. We discovered mutations in a new gene that we called secA ("sec" being short for secretion). Not only did mutations in this gene cause the β-galactosidase of our hybrid protein to return to the cytoplasm, but they also resulted in a cytoplasmic location for the normally exported maltose binding protein. And every other normally secreted protein we tested in the secA mutant was now in the cytoplasm! Once we had found the secA gene, it was a rather easy matter to determine what protein it encoded. These experiments led to a series of studies over the following years that identified a number of sec genes that specify the protein components of the secretion machinery. Others with a more biochemical bent (I had long since given up hope of successfully doing biochemistry) then were able to mix together Sec proteins with membrane preparations in a test tube and reconstitute the system that transferred proteins across membranes.

own New Guinea rivers in areas pop-
s.

pth how this enzyme, dsbA, worked,
alactosidase to MalF to select new mu-
ld find mutations that introduced dif-
nto dsbA and thus gain insight into the
In 1995, a graduate student, Hong-Ping
he genetic selection with the MalF–β-
so that we could detect mutations with
lfide bond formation. With the help of a
ine, Dana Boyd, she did obtain a collec-
red amino acids other than the cysteines
these yielded new insights into disulfide

mutants that Hong-Ping obtained we
affect disulfide bond formation at all. We
riginal purpose of Karen's mutant hunt—to
cted the assembly of proteins into the cell's
e that by designing a more sensitive ap-
nts in disulfide bond formation, we had also
mutations Karen McGovern had sought ten
as we realized this possibility, Hong-Ping
he mutations on the E. coli chromosome and
ected gene products involved in membrane
analysis showed that the mutations were in-
enes known to code for cellular components
ng membrane proteins to their place in the
ane. These mutations then proved useful for
nism of membrane protein insertion.
his project more than ten years earlier with the
g the mechanism that directs the assembly of
ytoplasmic membrane of E. coli. In the process,

We had now successfully used the gene fusion approach to define both the region within proteins that determined their secretion and some of the cellular components for getting such proteins
across membranes. Perhaps we could use the same gene fusion approach to study a related problem—the nature of the mechanism
responsible for assembling certain other proteins into the cytoplasmic membrane.

Membrane proteins of the bacteria are involved in many processes, including the transport of sugars and other molecules across
the membrane barrier into the cell. Such transport proteins include
one that is required for the accumulation of lactose in the cytoplasm (see Chapter 2) and two proteins that allow the cells to in-
ternalize the sugar maltose. So, this time, instead of fusing the gene
for β-galactosidase to that for a secreted protein, we fused it to a
gene for a membrane protein involved in maltose transport, MalF.
When we did this, we found the same result as with the maltose
binding protein–β-galactosidase fusion proteins. The MalF portion
of the hybrid protein inserted into the membrane and dragged β-
galactosidase after it. As a result, β-galactosidase was again stuck in
the membrane, where it was inactive and could no longer digest
lactose. This was exactly the property of the maltose binding protein–β-galactosidase fusions that had allowed us to find out so
much about protein secretion. We decided to go ahead and select
lac+ mutants of the MalF–β-galactosidase fusion that caused β-
galactosidase to return to the cytoplasm. We expected that such
mutations would include ones that cause defects in the components of the cell that guide proteins into the membrane. Then we
would have the tools to study the mechanism of membrane protein
assembly.

In 1987, a graduate student in the lab, Karen McGovern, took on
this project for her Ph.D. thesis. She readily obtained mutant deriv-
atives of the MalF–β-galactosidase fusion strain that could grow on

lactose. She showed that four of the mutations were in a gene on the E. coli chromosome distant from the site of the gene fusion. All four mutations altered the cell in such a way that the β-galactosidase was back in the cytoplasm, where it was active. We thought we had found a gene coding for a key cellular component involved in membrane protein assembly. For the next year, Karen attempted to prove that the product of this gene assisted the insertion of proteins into the cytoplasmic membrane. But her results led us to conclude that this gene was doing something very different in the cell. We had no idea what that something was. While this gene seemed very interesting, we could not predict how long it would take to find out what its product did in the bacteria. We decided that if Karen was going to complete a Ph.D. thesis, she would have to work on something that was more certain to yield concrete results. Karen, rather than risking another fruitless year, moved on to another project. We stored the mutant bacteria in our deep freezer.

It was not until four years later that we solved this problem. A new postdoctoral fellow, James Bardwell, arrived in the lab, and I offered him a choice of projects, including the option of following up on Karen's mutants. I warned him that it could be a wild goose chase. Jim thought that Karen's mutants looked interesting enough to take a chance on the project. He decided that the best course of action was to characterize the gene that was altered in Karen's mutants, in the hopes that this would tell us something about the function of the gene. He proceeded to locate the position of the gene on the chromosome, purify the gene away from the rest of the chromosomal material (gene cloning), and determine its DNA sequence. That DNA sequence allowed us, in turn, to deduce the sequence of amino acids in the protein. We found in the protein a sequence containing two cysteines arranged in a structure often found in enzymes that interact with disulfide bonds. We might never have recognized this pattern if we had not already been

in Madagascar and canoeing
ulated by head-hunting tribe
We wanted to study in d
using the same fusion of β-g
tants. We hoped that we wo
ferent amino acid changes i
functioning of the protein.
Tian, decided to modify
galactosidase fusion strain
more subtle effects on dis
long-time coworker of m
tion of mutations that alt
in the dsbA protein, and
bond formation.

However, among th
found some that did no
then remembered the o
find mutations that affe
membrane. Could it
proach to getting muta
picked up the kinds o
years earlier? As soo
proceeded to locate t
ask whether they af
protein assembly. He
deed alterations of
important for guidi
cytoplasmic memb
studying the mech
We had started
purpose of studyi
proteins into the

st
of
pri
very
agair
prote
sulfide
presen
lyst. W
disulfide
the gene
opened u
ing and be
my laborate

The succ
were interes
to recognize
would never
not been takei
them, and that
undertake a risk
piece with his te
gerous travels. Hi

we stumbled onto a whole new area of biology, the formation of disulfide bonds in proteins. In trying to probe more deeply into that area, we found ourselves unexpectedly back in the field of membrane protein assembly. In 1999, as Hong-Ping began to write up this last piece of work for publication, we decided to include some of the tortuous history of this project in the paper. This was not the usual way of presenting scientific results, but we felt that describing the actual course of events would in itself be instructive. We sent the manuscript for publication first to one and then to a second leading scientific journal. Our paper opened with a sentence which began: "This is the story . . ." Not unexpectedly, this style of writing was looked on with distaste by referees for the two journals:

> This section reads more like a personal memoir than a formal presentation of background information.

> The introduction is a bit "fairy tale like."

> This manuscript is written in the exotic style of a story.

The paper was rejected by both journals, although the stylistic issue may not have been the main reason. Ultimately, having received strongly favorable comments from other scientists, I published the paper in the *Proceedings of the National Academy of Sciences*. I am a member of the Academy and publication in this journal is virtually guaranteed for members who assure the editors that the paper has received approval from other scientists.

▲ ▲ ▲ Our decision to prepare this manuscript as a story exemplifies the integration of my interest in the history, philosophy, and social consequences of science with my own scientific research. I had come to see how the scientific process is idealized by its portrayal in school texts and by the image of it purveyed by the media.

For those university students who enter scientific careers, the mode of presenting research in scientific journals further strengthens the myth of a pure objective science.

Scientists, of course, may argue that there is beauty and creativity in telling the tale of a scientific achievement as though it were a product of human logic from its inception to its conclusion. Such a picture of the scientific process may not reflect reality, but it offers to its readers an image of how science could ideally proceed. Presented in this way, with clean lines and an orderly flow of compelling argumentation, science can inspire. My own reading of the articles of Jacob and Monod that epitomized this style—the reconstruction of a process of intuition, chance, and revelation to fit the language of logic—had been an important experience in my decision to become—and stay—a scientist. The French scientists' perfecting of this mode of presentation no doubt had its roots in their country's educational system, where logic is emphasized from a very early age.

Yet interesting scientific discoveries are rarely the product of such a linear process. The misrepresentation of the workings of science leaves out the human elements, the wrong turns, the surprises, the flashes of intuition, even the passions that drive us in science. It also fails to acknowledge the biases, the assumptions that we all must start with in order to proceed in a scientific investigation.

One consequence of this romanticized but seamless picture is to place science on a higher pedestal than it warrants. If the process is as perfected as scientific papers would have it, science and the scientists would indeed deserve a good deal of trust. While I certainly believe that a rational approach to scientific problems is an ideal to be sought, the actual practice of science is a human endeavor with the flaws and virtues of any human activity. Science's undeservedly high pedestal allows its practitioners to present presumed insights into human behavior and social arrangements as though they represented objective truth. At least, the media and the public take them that way. When the story of the super-aggressive XYY male was first reported, it not only attracted widespread media attention, but also quickly became incorporated as gospel into most textbooks of high school biology, college psychology, medical school genetics, and psychiatry. When the validity of the "criminal chromosome" story was strongly questioned several years later, the "story" was dropped from these texts. Only permanent truths would remain in the sources of scientific knowledge—at least, as long as they too would persist as "true." Wouldn't it make far more sense to leave these "stories" and their subsequent retraction in the texts as a tool to help students understand and appreciate how science really works? To describe the curiously tangled course of the XYY controversy? To show where scientists can go wrong and what factors, what underlying assumptions, lead to poorly done studies and erroneous conclusions?

Old discarded "truths" are almost always eliminated from texts and hidden from the public so that only the clean, unchallenged lines of argument remain. As a result, the next time a scientist announces to the public the discovery that men have a rape gene, or that people's tendencies to take risks are genetically predetermined, the report will gain immediate currency, wreak social havoc or not, and then, soon after, disappear again from our truths. Science is more interesting than that.

▲ ▲ ▲ Our chance discovery of how disulfide bonds are formed took one more unexpected turn—this time one involving the intersection of science and ethics. Soon after we published our first papers on this subject, scientists from academia and biotechnology companies began to contact us. They hoped that our understanding of disulfide bond formation and the bacterial strains that we had developed might aid them in their own work. The biotechnology companies were in the business of making large quantities of medically useful substances, often using E. coli as a protein "factory." Some of the proteins they made contained disulfide bonds: hormones such as insulin, drugs used to treat heart disease such as tissue plasminogen activator, and antibodies that help humans fight infections and perhaps even cancer. The E. coli strains we were developing might be useful for increasing the amounts of proteins that could be harvested.

I was approached by a research group leader from Genentech, one of the first and most successful of the biotechnology companies. James Swartz invited me to visit his South San Francisco laboratories and talk to his group about our research on disulfide bonds. At the same time, he asked if I would act as a scientific consultant to his group. I said yes to the first invitation and no to the second. I had for years refused requests to act as a consultant. If I was to remain a critic of practices within the genetics community I did not want to have any ties that might subtly influence my independence. Although I had been a member of the Scientific Advisory Board to the company New England BioLabs, I felt that my association with that company did not violate my ethics. The president of that company, Donald Comb, was progressive both in his politics and in his company policies: a high degree of profit-sharing, a daycare center, funding of research on understudied third world diseases, and establishment of the New England BioLabs Foundation, which supports progressive political causes.

In 1994, soon after my first trip to Genentech, Jim Swartz asked me again if I would be a consultant. This time I said yes. I found my interactions with Jim and his group enjoyable and mutually beneficial. Then, as though by natural design, thunder struck. On the very week that I signed the contract, a front-page New York Times article exposed unethical practices by Genentech.

The genetically engineered production of human growth hormone (a disulfide bond–containing protein) was one of Genentech's early successes. Protropin, the trade name given their product, relieved many of the problems suffered by children with a genetically based form of dwarfism resulting from a deficiency in the production of the hormone. Without treatment, the children are extremely short and suffer other health problems. But the number of children born with these genetic conditions is very small, insufficient to generate much revenue for Genentech. Apparently for these reasons, Caremark, a company that distributed the drug for Genentech, was aggressively marketing the hormone to doctors and to families of children who were shorter than the average, even though there was no evidence that Protropin would increase the height of children other than those with the specific genetic deficiencies. In some cases, doctors associated with Caremark made connections with school classrooms, where short children were identified, and then contacted their parents. Apparently, the doctors tried to persuade parents that they would be neglecting their child if they didn't offer Protropin treatment. One mother said that a doctor projected her son's eventual height as five feet, six inches and then asked her what she would say to her son when he grew up and learned that "he could have been five-ten." The New York Times reported that a grand jury had indicted one of the doctors and a vice president of Genentech.

I was faced with a dilemma. Should I break my contract with Genentech or use my connection to express my strong opposition to this practice? I decided on the latter course. I called up Jim Swartz and said that I wanted to talk with a high-level official in the organization. He put me in touch with the vice president for research, Arthur Levinson, telling him to take my concerns seriously—"we really want to keep Beckwith as a consultant." I wrote and spoke to Levinson expressing my dismay, suggesting that the company establish an "ethics" board that would monitor such marketing practices. I thought also of contacting other academic consultants to the company to urge them to express their discontent. That proved a difficult task because the list of consultants was not public information. The following year, Genentech's president, G. Kirk Raab, was forced to resign; the company's methods in marketing Protropin were cited as one of the factors. Arthur Levinson replaced him.

I have no idea whether my comments had any effect at all; the complaints of one person are unlikely to carry much weight. But my experience brought home to me how much power scientists might have if they were to couple their positions as consultants with an effort to monitor the unethical or exploitive practices of the companies they advise. In this case, Genentech, in order to increase its sales, was, in effect, medicalizing short stature, trying to persuade consumers that this was a defect that should be medically treated. This practice exemplified the fears that many of us have about the impact of the new genetics; in the rush by drug companies to profit from new genetic tests and products, much social damage could be done. The issues ELSI had been studying, genetic discrimination, stigmatization, psychological harm, and medicalization of social problems, had all been documented. Don't geneticists who have contributed to the development of these tests and products have a responsibility to ensure that their work is used to benefit, not harm, people?

CHAPTER 12

Geneticists and the Two Cultures

I started out in science with a split personality. The world of ideas outside of science attracted me, but it seemed so separate from the world within the scientific community. Over the years, the two worlds gradually came together for me. My political involvement merged with my life in science. My readings in philosophy, history, and sociology of science influenced my own scientific research. My awareness of the nonobjective factors that enter into the scientific process gave me new ways to look at the successes and the failures, the wrong turns and the lucky breaks, the assumptions that I brought to my work. I learned to step back from the science and muse over the wonderfully human effort that it is.

The gap that I had felt early in my career mirrored the long-standing gulf between scientists and people working in other fields —a gulf that still exists. Later in my career, my experiences with the ELSI Working Group of the Human Genome Project (HGP) heightened my awareness of the mutual distrust between the two camps, a disheartening situation.

▲ ▲ ▲ In 1989, when Jim Watson commissioned the members of the ELSI group to explore the potential adverse consequences of human genome sequencing, we were asked to foresee the likely problems raised by the HGP and suggest how the available funds could be directed to evaluate the problems and devise means of preventing them. We could also establish our own task forces to deal with problems that seemed imminent enough to require immediate attention.

The ELSI Working Group first met at the NIH in Bethesda, Maryland, in September of 1989. Five of its seven members were trained in science. The chair, Nancy Wexler, with a Ph.D. in psychology, had worked closely with geneticists in the effort to map the Huntington's gene. Victor McKusick, a geneticist from Johns Hopkins University, was considered the father of human genetics. His book *Mendelian Inheritance in Man* was widely used as the source of information on the human genome and its 4,000 mapped genes. McKusick also served as chair of the internationally based Human Genome Organization's ethics committee. Robert Murray, a clinical geneticist at Howard University, had written for many years on issues related to sickle cell genetic screening. Together with Dr. James Bowman of the University of Chicago, he had published the book *Genetic Variation and Disorders in Peoples of African Origin*. Thomas Murray, trained in social psychology, was well known for his commentaries on ethical issues in medicine and medical research. Head of a medical ethics program at Case Western Reserve University in 1989, he later became president of the Hastings Center for Bioethics in Hastings-on-Hudson, New York, the leading think tank on bioethics issues in the United States. Patricia King, a lawyer and Georgetown University law professor, wrote on the social ramifications of medical and genetic research, especially those involving issues of race. She had been a member of government commissions formed to explore bioethics topics. Robert Cook-Deegan, after earning a medical degree and pursuing biomedical postdoctoral research, had switched to health policy issues. His reports on gene therapy and on the genome project led to his appointment as acting director of a congressional bioethics commission.

The NIH and DOE wings of the Human Genome Project provided the Working Group with a small staff and advisors, including Eric Juengst, a philosopher who had written on biomedical ethics issues, and Michael Yesley, a lawyer with the DOE's Los Alamos facility, who had been the staff director of the earlier National Commission for the Protection of Human Subjects of Biomedical and Behavioral Research from 1974 to 1978.

With the group so heavily weighted toward the sciences, it might appear that NIH had simply appointed the foxes to guard the chicken coop; the group had been established by a geneticist, Jim Watson; its funds depended on Watson, the HGP scientific council, and the NIH; and nearly every one of its meetings (three or four a year) was held at or near the NIH. Several of us, however, were known for taking public and even adversarial stands against the misuse of genetic information. Furthermore, no explicit restrictions limited the issues we might explore. Perhaps most important for the group's independence, Jim Watson essentially left us to our own devices. Over the five years I served with the ELSI Working Group, Jim came to perhaps one or two of its meetings. As far as I can tell, he never interfered with any of our activities. Funding was available for whatever projects we deemed important. Our major complaint was the small number of staff.

Some activist friends criticized my decision to join the Working Group, arguing that I was being used as a front to give the illusion that scientists were being responsible. They contended, for example, that there was no way the Working Group could suggest that the Human Genome Project be stopped because of its potential social consequences. Maybe yes, maybe no. But this question was not an issue for me. Although I had expressed objections to the funding of HGP for fear of its effects on basic genetic research, I did not object to it on the basis of the social dangers that I foresaw. I had long since rejected the idea that the best way to prevent the harmful results of scientific developments was to stop the progress of science. At any rate, the cat was out of the bag, since human genetics had been proceeding rapidly for some time before the Human Genome Project began. The problems that the HGP might exacerbate were before us whether or not the HGP continued. Here was at least hope that we could confront issues already raised by progress in genetics.

The ELSI Working Group launched two efforts. First, we developed an agenda for the several-million-dollar program of research on ELSI issues. The Human Genome Project should fund research and conferences to investigate a range of critical topics, including: (1) fairness in the use of genetic information; (2) the impact of genetic information on the individual, including such issues as stigmatization and psychological responses; (3) the privacy and confidentiality of genetic information; (4) the consequences of the HGP for genetic counseling; (5) the influence of genetic information on reproductive decisions; (6) the impact of introducing genetics into mainstream clinical practice; (7) historical analysis of the misuses of genetics in the past and their contemporary relevance; (8) the issue of free will and other conceptual and philosophical implications of the HGP; and (9) the influence of commercialization of the products of the HGP. In addition, we proposed that the NIH and DOE wings of the HGP should fund public education projects that not only explained the science but also raised ELSI issues.

Given the grant awarding process, the pace of academic research, and the complicated nature of many of the questions, we recognized that the ELSI-funded research projects would take years to yield their conclusions. Yet some of these issues required more immediate attention. Human genome research's major contribution to medicine in the near future would be the pinpointing of genes connected with human disease. Developing a detailed genetic map of human chromosomes and ultimately the complete human genome sequence would vastly increase the ability to identify such genes. Using genetic tests, doctors would be able to predict who would be susceptible to any one of a whole range of health problems.

We decided to elaborate on three crucial concerns raised by this anticipated increase in genetic information. First: Would the health insurance industry want or have access to genetic test results in order to make decisions about access to insurance for individuals who had been tested? If so, how should society deal with the potential harm that might result? Second: How would the ever increasing genetic information about individuals be used by employers, schools, and other social institutions? How much privacy should be afforded that information? Third: How would both health professionals and the public, each little schooled in the concepts of genetics, cope with this new genetic knowledge? The ability to identify people who were susceptible to health problems would generate a vast new source of information for practitioners and clients of the health care system.

To investigate the insurance issue, the ELSI Working Group established a task force co-chaired by Tom Murray and me. Our committee included geneticists, representatives of the insurance industry and consumer groups, and sociologists who studied the health care system. We met for two years and issued our report early in 1993. We addressed two issues. First, we focused on the very real possibility that large numbers of people would have problems obtaining health insurance because of the increasing use of genetic tests. Even people who showed no signs of illness could lose their coverage because of a test that indicated susceptibility to a disease that might never materialize.

Second, despite these concerns, we recognized that for society to single out genetic tests for special protection was problematic. We pointed out the substantial overlap between health problems that have been called genetic and those that have environmental causes. It is rare to find a disease that is completely determined by genetics. AIDS is unquestionably an environmental disease, but a small fraction of the population is genetically resistant to the virus. Individuals who are susceptible to heart disease because of their genetic makeup can improve their health prospects through diet and exercise. We argued that there are both environmental and genetic components responsible for most health conditions. Furthermore, there are many nongenetic medical tests that, like genetic tests, can predict susceptibility to disease in those who are perfectly healthy. For instance, a chemical test for high cholesterol levels provides warning of potential heart problems. Because of this overlap, we concluded that offering privacy privileges for genetic tests and not for other types of predictive tests did not make sense from a scientific or medical perspective.

We predicted that the continuing increase in genetic testing would eventually raise complex questions for the health insurance system. Since all people carry mutations that make them susceptible to one or another health problem, the ultimate identification of all these mutations would make a mockery of the underwriting practices of the insurance industry. If everyone were at risk and that risk could be defined, each person would be charged an insurance rate (or refused insurance) on the basis of his or her genetic makeup. Our report argued that such a consequence of increased genetic testing presented a strong rationale for a national health system. We felt comfortable with this conclusion because our report was completed early in the Clinton administration when it appeared that the country was well on its way to a national health plan. In fact, Hillary Clinton, after talking with Nancy Wexler, used our report as an added argument for the administration's health plan. What we didn't foresee was the rapid and surprising loss of momentum and ultimate crashing of the universal health care efforts.

Independently of our Health Insurance Task Force, the Working Group supported funding of a group of researchers who would take up more generally the issue of the privacy of genetic information. Decisions about the extent of privacy protections required the input of lawyers, philosophers, and economists who investigated fundamental questions about principles of privacy and their relationship to genetic privacy in particular. Michael Yesley coordinated regular meetings of the researchers. The deliberate and often philosophical discussions of principle that seemed essential to these analyses were to increase the misgivings of genome scientists about ELSI's work. This grumbling continued even though a model privacy law eventually materialized from this project that was to provide the basis for proposed congressional acts.

Finally, we commissioned a report from the Institute of Medicine (IOM), published in 1994 under the title *Assessing Genetic Risk*, which evaluated the consequences of the introduction of genetic testing into the clinical setting. But even before the report appeared, problems were emerging. As commercial interests sought to reap the benefits of human genome research, genetic tests became the first marketable products. We were concerned that a rush to introduce these tests could lead to significant harm to clients of the health care system. The first test case was cystic fibrosis (CF), the most common recessive genetic disease among the majority Caucasian population in the United States. Some biotechnology companies and private clinics, foreseeing a large market, were pushing for population-wide CF screening.

Because of the immediacy of the CF issue, we convened a series of workshops attended by CF researchers, ethicists, and representatives of cystic fibrosis patient support groups. We discussed the problems that would likely arise from widespread CF screening: The CF genetic test could not give precise predictions, and so in many cases it would lead to confusion, uncertainty, and, given past experience, psychological problems among those tested. There were only 800 genetic counselors in the country; consumers would be counseled by doctors, most of whom were untrained in the communication of genetic information. We came to quick agreement that there should be a moratorium on population-wide screening. We funded pilot studies to determine the best means of ensuring consumers' understanding of CF tests and to assess the seriousness of any problems that might arise from testing. Our initiatives, in conjunction with those of a National Institutes of Health consensus meeting and the American Society of Human Genetics, led to effective public calls for limiting CF screening to those families where there was a history of the disease. The Working Group later took the same overall approach to evaluating screening for mutations in the BRCA1 and BRCA2 genes—mutations that conferred susceptibility to breast and ovarian cancer. The medical community maintained the position on CF testing for ten years, until some groups broke rank in 2001, suggesting that the test be offered to the entire population.

▲ ▲ ▲ Our handling of the CF issue exemplifies the importance of the ELSI Working Group. Having a knowledgeable and concerned group thinking about these issues, and prepared to deal with problems as they arose, was a stimulus leading other organizations to become involved. In the absence of ELSI, it is not clear that actions such as those taken to deal with CF screening would ever have materialized.

The Working Group also acted to influence the impact of the Americans with Disabilities Act of 1991 on genetic issues. We succeeded in convincing the EEOC (Equal Employment Opportunity

Commission) that it should take into account genetic test information in writing the regulations for this law. We argued that, without privacy regulations, many individuals would be rejected for or lose employment as a result of an employer's foreknowledge of genetic test results. The EEOC agreed with us and ruled to include genetic test results among the kinds of medical information that employers were forbidden to use in hiring decisions.

While the ELSI Working Group explored several of these crucial issues, NIH committees were doling out 3–5 percent of the HGP budget for grants that implemented the actions we had outlined. These grants supported educational efforts ranging from high school biology curricula that explained the Human Genome Project and its social implications to television programs outlining the science and social issues of genome research. ELSI also funded projects to assess the impact of genetic information on people who had undergone genetic tests. Studies in clinical settings examined the consumer's understanding and responses to genetic test results. Surveys, including the one carried out by the Genetic Screening Study Group, investigated the issue of genetic discrimination. ELSI funded projects by philosophers, sociologists, ethicists, and historians to examine a whole range of issues related to the social impact of genetic information. A number of these projects led to conferences and books, many of which have become important sources for the analysis of the social and ethical questions associated with the Human Genome Project.

Some genome scientists who were critical of the ELSI program labeled it a "welfare project" for researchers in the social sciences. These same critics would never have considered the Human Genome Project a welfare project for geneticists. At any rate, ELSI's achievements put the lie to that evaluation. In addition to material products and even legislative consequences, this "welfare project" helped raise public awareness and understanding of genetics and its social ramifications through support of educational materials, television programs, and books and conferences. Furthermore, ELSI's "welfare recipients" became important resources for members of the media when they sought knowledgeable commentators on the meaning and implications of new genetic reports. Such reports were appearing with ever increasing frequency. In fact, the unprecedented nature of the ELSI project—the melding of social concerns with the very beginning of a scientific project—is now considered by some a model for how to launch scientific endeavors in the future. The success of ELSI's many projects may be secondary to the principle it established.

The scientific wing of the Human Genome Project did not share this positive view of ELSI's achievements. Not long after ELSI was established, genome scientists on the project began to grumble. ELSI Working Group members became increasingly aware of their hostility. We heard of and read in the media disparaging personal comments that continued during the seven-year life-span of the Working Group.

> Eric Juengst heard an NIH official complain, "I still don't understand why you want to spend all this money subsidizing the vacuous pronunciamentos of self-styled ethicists."

> Francis Collins, who succeeded Jim Watson as director of the HGP, said that "some of the science types looked on ELSI as a 'welfare program' for ethicists, who only talked, but didn't change the world."

> David Botstein, a member of the HGP's scientific council, spoke of "the prurient speculation that has a tendency to excite everybody's ELSI instincts."

> "Some bench scientists are openly fed up. 'We've had enough of this Hastings Center stuff,' said one [genome scientist]."

Maynard Olson, head of a genome unit at the University of Washington asked, "Why don't we have any visible progress toward a federal privacy law three years into the program?"

Many genome scientists seemed to look on the ELSI program and the Working Group as a "soft science" project unworthy of their respect, even though five of our seven members were trained as biological or biomedical scientists. I found myself occasionally forgetting that I was a scientist, now that I was identified with the "vacuous" ethicists.

Late in 1993 the ELSI Working Group expanded. The pediatric geneticist Neil (Tony) Holtzman of Johns Hopkins Medical School, author of *Proceed with Caution*, a book that warns of problems associated with genetic screening, and David Cox, a member of the Stanford University Genome Project, joined the group. We also recruited the sociologists Dorothy Nelkin and Troy Duster and the lawyer Lori Andrews, all of whom had written on ethical and social issues in genetics. Marsha Saxton, a strong advocate for the disabled who was born with spina bifida, and Joe McInerney, whose BSCS (Biological Sciences Curriculum Study) center in Colorado published high school curricular modules on the genome, rounded out the reinvigorated group. Those of us who had started with the Working Group in 1989 would rotate off over the next two years.

Also in 1993, Jim Watson resigned the directorship of the HGP and was replaced by Francis Collins, one of the leaders in human genome mapping efforts. Collins's research group had participated in the location of the genes responsible for cystic fibrosis and some cases of breast cancer (BRCA1). Collins quickly showed that he planned to take a more active role in ELSI affairs. He attended many of our meetings and participated in the discussion of ethical issues.

Shortly after the changes at ELSI, a major public controversy arose over new genetic claims that were reminiscent of the eugenics period. The psychologist Richard Herrnstein and the political scientist Charles Murray argued in their book, The Bell Curve (1994), that in the United States people with genes for lower intelligence and for antisocial traits were outbreeding those with better genes. These supposed "dysgenic" trends, they contended, were the root cause of social problems such as crime and unemployment. To remedy these problems, the authors proposed that welfare and remedial education programs be ended and that women from the upper classes be encouraged by new social programs to bear more children. The book received immediate and widespread media attention.

The ELSI Working Group thought that the genome community should respond to The Bell Curve for two reasons: First, we believed that the book's authors had misused genetic concepts and supported their argument with highly questionable genetic evidence. And second, at the same time, we thought that the deterministic view of genetics that Herrnstein and Murray presented had been strengthened by public statements of scientists who were involved with the Human Genome Project. Major figures in the establishment of the genome project had made grand claims for the power of genetics, perhaps to maintain public support for the HGP. Jim Watson stated to Time magazine: "We used to think our fate was in our stars. Now we know, in large measure, our fate is in our genes." The Harvard biologist Walter Gilbert suggested that the human genome sequence would yield "the ultimate explanation of a human being." The DOE scientist Charles DeLisi referred to the human genome as "The Blueprint for Life" and the geneticist Robert Sinsheimer claimed that the sequence "defines a human being."

We feared that genome scientists, through their public statements, were creating an environment in which genetic determinist claims appeared to carry science's stamp of approval. We felt strongly that the Human Genome Project should counter Herrnstein and Murray's misrepresentation of genetics and clearly dissociate the HGP from such genetic determinist views of the world and its social arrangements. The ELSI Working Group put together a response to *The Bell Curve*, intending to move quickly to publish it.

In this same period, we continued our efforts to anticipate other issues arising out of human genome research that required attention. The appearance of *The Bell Curve* took place in the midst of a raft of reports on genes for human behaviors. First-line scientific journals published studies that described the mapping of genes associated with manic depressive illness, schizophrenia, homosexuality, risk-taking, happiness, autism, dyslexia, and more. Even though many of these reports were subsequently challenged or retracted, the media coverage was extensive and, generally, uncritical. Research in human behavioral genetics and its social consequences lay at the heart of ELSI concerns as we had originally described them. Many of the unfortunate social consequences emanating from genetics, going back to the eugenics era, had been closely connected with studies of behavioral genetics. If the HGP was to take seriously its mandate to anticipate the consequences of the project, this subject was certainly high on the list of issues to consider. We asked for funds to begin examination of the implications of behavioral genetics research.

This series of events—Francis Collins's arrival as director of the HGP, our statement on *The Bell Curve*, and our request for funds to support analysis of the social impact of human behavioral genetics—proved to be a critical turning point for the ELSI Working Group. More than most scientists, Collins was seriously concerned about the social consequences of the HGP. Yet rather then letting the ELSI Working Group prioritize issues, he insisted that we put our efforts into the problem that he felt was the most important, privacy. Collins found "too mushy" projects such as ELSI analysis of the psychological impact on people of genetic test results. His assumption of a guiding role in ELSI issues appeared to reflect the dissatisfaction of genome scientists with the ELSI program. No more "soft science," "prurient speculation," or "vacuous pronunciamentos of self-styled ethicists."

Relations between the ELSI Working Group and the scientific wing of the HGP rapidly deteriorated. Collins's staff delayed publication of our statement on *The Bell Curve* for an inordinate amount of time. It finally appeared in the *American Journal of Human Genetics* in 1996, two years after the publication of the Herrnstein-Murray book. Funds were withdrawn for our study of human behavioral genetics. The actions of Collins and his staff undermined the quasi-independence of ELSI. The supposed advantages of an ELSI integrated into the scientific project had been compromised. Would the foxes now guard the chicken coop? Coincidentally, just as antagonism was increasing between the ELSI Working Group and the scientific wing of HGP, the founding members of the group, including Nancy Wexler and me, were rotated off. Lori Andrews took over the chair from Nancy. The role of the Working Group declined even further as the number of its meetings was reduced to one a year, which eliminated the possibility of functioning effectively. Faced with the loss of independence, Lori Andrews resigned as chair in 1996. Collins disbanded the Working Group and reconstituted a committee of his own choosing.

I had begun my tenure on the ELSI Working Group with high hopes. In the first few years, with a small staff and only a few meetings a year, we had accomplished a lot. Why then did we encounter such antagonism from genome scientists? Admittedly, scientists were unused to having a watchdog within their own project, albeit a watchdog that wasn't threatening its master—at least, as far as we could see. The reaction of the genome scientists may simply have been another manifestation of the age-old gap between the scientific community and those in the humanities and social sciences. Hard scientists' lack of respect for the "soft sciences" caused them to mistrust the project from its inception. Jim Watson, even though he created ELSI, did not expect or hope for much action from the Working Group. Lori Andrews reports in her book, *The Clone Age*, that Watson stated at a genetics policy meeting, "I wanted a group that would talk and talk and never get anything done, and if they did something, I wanted them to get it wrong. I wanted as its head Shirley Temple Black."

Genome scientists may have been impatient with ELSI's progress because they expected that the complex process of developing social policy could be achieved with the same efficiency as scientific accomplishments. "Why don't we have any visible progress toward a federal privacy law three years into the program?" Scientists have a can-do attitude. We are used to solving technical problems very quickly. We set up experiments in the lab with a fairly certain idea of how long they will take. We finish them, write up the conclusions, and publish perhaps three, five, or ten papers a year. The idea that a "simple" issue such as the development of privacy guidelines and legislation could require a few years of research and thought by experts on legal, philosophical, economic, ethical, and other matters did not fit the scientific mind-set.

The genome scientists may also have feared that ELSI activities would interfere with their science. Our analysis of human behavioral genetics and its impact may have been seen as an attack on the research itself. I had repeatedly encountered this response in my own career as an activist within science. From the reaction of my colleagues during the XYY controversy to the science-antiscience false dichotomy of the sociobiology debate, any word of criticism elicited surprising anxiety. Scientists and the media repeatedly compared criticism to the seventeenth-century Catholic church's attack on Galileo. No one on the ELSI Working Group took a position against the science: there was never any discussion of preventing research.

Our Working Group could have been more active in trying to bridge the gap; we did not keep close contact with the people who held the purse strings. Yet, in retrospect, the gulf seems to have been so wide that it is unlikely such meetings would have bridged it.

Blame for the communication failure cannot be attributed to the geneticists alone. Problems exist on both sides of the divide. Some who write and speak on the ethical and social issues often stray beyond their understanding of the science. I have winced through lectures by ethicists talking about the implications of a particular genetic development that they misrepresented or misunderstood. Geneticists can then easily dismiss comments from this other world because of the limited scientific knowledge of the ethicists. But just as there is much badly done social and ethical analysis, there is much badly done science. Glib analyses from the ELSI side and contemptuous attitudes and responses from the scientists don't help. We need each other; it is only from interactions and collaboration between these two worlds and with the public that ELSI problems can be dealt with.

▲ ▲ ▲ After my ultimately disappointing experience in ELSI, I reread C. P. Snow's Two Cultures. I wanted insight into the lack of communication between scientists and those in other disciplines. Snow opens his famous "Rede Lecture" in an even-handed way, pointing out both the failure of scientists to expand their cultural breadth and the lack of scientific knowledge among those in the humanities. He complains, "I felt I was moving among two groups, who had almost ceased to communicate at all, who, in intellectual, moral and psychological climate, had so little in common that instead of going from Burlington House of South Kensington to Chelsea, one might have crossed an ocean." But he quickly changes tack, progressively putting more and more of the blame on those in the humanities. As the historian Graham Burnett puts it, "He left no doubt that, in his view, the burden of responsibility fell heavily on the literary culture." Snow even goes on to suggest that there is a "moral component right in the grain of science itself."

This claim for the moral authority of science irked me. I remembered the same attitude being expressed by Jacques Monod in his book, *Chance and Necessity*. Monod argued that there is an "ethic of objectivity" inherent in science—and that this ethic offered the basis for a new belief system, replacing religion and political philosophies as the foundation of society. I had been surprised to see these scientistic statements coming from one of my scientific heroes. Monod's own scientific work was infused with many nonobjective components—intuitions, leaps, invocations of the "beauty" of a theory as justification for its acceptance. How could he make such strong claims for the pure objectivity of science in the face of his own scientific method? As the British philosopher David Miller puts it, with evident irony, "If scientists would [only] stop overlauding scientific rationality in the face of reason."

I could not accept Snow's analysis. Even though in college in the 1950s I had experienced the snobbishness of the literary culture toward scientists that Snow describes, I had also experienced the insularity and narrowness of the scientific community. Today, with the ascendancy of science, leading scientists too often exhibit a kind of triumphalism at finding themselves so well funded and honored in society. The tables have been turned; it's the scientists' chance to be the snobs.

I realized that the sad trajectory of the ELSI program was part of the long history of conflict between these two worlds. Lionel

Trilling notes a striking resemblance between the "two cultures" debate started by Snow in 1959 and the nineteenth-century debates between Thomas Huxley and Matthew Arnold, the one arguing for the ascendancy of science, the other decrying the socially destructive aspects of science and technology. The recent "Science Wars" controversy provoked by the physicist Norman Levitt and the biologist Paul Gross pitted natural scientists against academics working in what they called "cultural studies of science." Gross and Levitt's book *Higher Superstition* (1994) argued that the thrust of the "cultural" analyses downgraded the image of science, putting its methodology in the same ranks as that of any other field. They worried about the damage to science, the possible fueling of anti-science trends among the public, and the loss of science funding. Even at a time of dramatically increased funding of science, scientists again took criticism or just plain analysis as a threat to "scientific progress." Since there were easy targets among the cultural studies folk—the ethicist or sociologist who got the science wrong—the two scientists readily found horror stories among the writings of people in the "cultural" camp and, as a result, dismissed the entire field.

Gross and Levitt saw little or no value in the analysis of the scientific world by those who were not themselves scientists. They went so far as to propose that scientists should play a role in the decisions of academic tenure committees for nonscientific departments whenever a candidate's work dealt with science. They rejected the complementary suggestion that nonscientists have the right to be part of tenure committees in the sciences. I don't see why both practices shouldn't be considered. They suggested that if a university humanities department happened to disband, scientists, with their own broad knowledge, could easily repopulate that department from their own ranks.

The "Science Wars" continue with books, debates over academic appointments in major universities, and one cause célèbre. Stimulated by reading *Higher Superstition*, the physicist Alan Sokal played an elaborate hoax on the "cultural" side. Sokal composed an attack on scientific objectivity, following the line of certain postmodern analyses and using language from quantum physics to support his thesis. He purposefully constructed a nonsensical argument, masked by the complex "discourse" of quantum theory, and sent it for publication to a leading journal in the "cultural studies" field. The journal, *Social Text*, published the article without any changes. Sokal then publicly exposed the hoax, proclaiming it was evidence for the vacuousness of the entire field of cultural studies of science.

These controversies do highlight real issues in the long-standing "Two Cultures" conflict. On the one side we have the unwarranted triumphalism of Thomas Huxley, of C. P. Snow, of Jacques Monod, of Paul Gross and Norman Levitt, of certain genome scientists, who exalt science as an endeavor above human foibles, as the only rational source for informing social policy. Science, beyond its practical applications, does have much to offer society—the qualities of skepticism, openness to new arguments, the testing of theories against evidence, even the beauty of discovery. But it is not the all-knowing or the only source we should look to for life instruction. The myth of complete objectivity often masks a host of personal or political agendas that influence the doing of science and its presentation to the public. The nonobjective factors, such as personal, social, and ideological prejudices, simple passion, and dogged or even blind commitment, and financial interests, are often as important in the genesis and realization of scientific advances as the "rules" of controlled experiments, the testing of a theory's predictions, and willingness to consider peer criticism.

On the other side of the debate we have those in the "cultural studies" field who study science from the outside and who describe the subjective and cultural components of scientific inquiry. Sometimes they take their analysis to the extreme. Some of their critiques appear to challenge the right of science to have any more validity than even the most mystical of human endeavors.

It is my belief that if we are to solve the social dilemmas associated with scientific research, these two "cultures" must work together, each of them open to the perspectives of the other. My experience in the early years of existence of the ELSI Working Group at the NIH and with the Genetic Screening Study Group in Boston gives me optimism that such efforts can succeed. (A remarkable effort to bridge the two-culture gap can be found in a series of essays in the recent book *The One Culture: A Conversation about Science*, edited by Jay A. Labinger, a chemist, and Harry Collins, a sociologist.)

Students, researchers, and teachers in sociology, law, ethics, and the natural sciences have collaborated in the Genetic Screening Study Group for years. We discuss articles related to the social impact of genetics, not only monitoring those in scientific, sociological, and philosophy journals, but also analyzing the popular media's presentation of genetics. We organize conferences, speak out at other forums, and press for public policies that confront problems generated by the increasing availability of genetic information. We learn from one another to appreciate different approaches to examining genetics-related social problems and to devising possible solutions. We critique one another's papers from our different perspectives, immensely enriching the thinking of all of us. Those in our group not versed in genetics learn how to distinguish genetic reality from fantasy, how to assess the validity of genetic research itself. The scientists among us gain new perspectives on the social context of science—how that context influences science and how science affects real people.

The meeting of the "two cultures" is not an easy one. Each group I have worked in has had difficulties in communicating. Nevertheless, science is too big a part of our lives today to leave the thinking to scientists alone.

CHAPTER 13

The Scientist and the Quail Farmer

I began this book by recounting my visit with François Williams, the scientist turned political activist, the activist turned quail farmer and successful village mayor. In his stone farmhouse in Normandy, we traced the course of our lives since our lab partner days at Harvard in the 1950s. We discovered remarkable similarities in our paths toward and away from science. Our discussions prompted me to ask myself what I had achieved by my choices. Was I right in telling François that some of us had been able to bring into science a social and ethical perspective that affected the impact of scientific developments? There is no clear answer to this question.

Atomic physicists, through their political actions in the 1950s and 1960s, had probably influenced nuclear weapons policy; the extent of their effect is not clear. The situation is even murkier when it comes to genetics. Since the 1960s, there have certainly been changes in attitudes toward social activism among practitioners of the biological sciences, both students and older scientists. In 1969, geneticists responded to Arthur Jensen's widely publicized claims of a connection between genes, race, and intelligence, perhaps with enough force to blunt some of the social impact of

his report. Still, only a handful of geneticists made public their refutations of this misuse and misrepresentation of genetics—a small
number compared to the group of physicists who mobilized in the
1950s and 1960s.

In the mid-1970s, several prominent geneticists recognized the
need to consider the impact of science when they urged caution in
proceeding with recombinant DNA research, proposing a moratorium on certain experiments. I believe that the steps taken by this
group are traceable to the scientific activism of younger geneticists
in the preceding few years. The recombinant DNA controversy, un-
fortunately, deteriorated into bitter squabbling among scientists as
the public became more involved in the issues. Some of the scientists who had called for the moratorium worried subsequently that
taking such a stance publicly was a threat to scientific progress.

Although the development of the recombinant DNA technique
catalyzed debates over social responsibility in science, the technology itself contributed to a decline in activism. Within a few years
of the 1973 call for caution, the new power to manipulate DNA fueled the beginning of the biotechnology industry. Geneticists, including many of those who had been politically involved, accepted
positions as scientific advisors to biotechnology companies or
started their own. Their involvement in profit-making institutions
incorporated them more strongly into a system that they had until
then been able to stand apart from. The additional traveling and
consulting entailed by such ventures combined with their own laboratory work left little time for other activities.

Nevertheless, it did seem that the ethical and social implications
of genetics could no longer be ignored by the community of geneticists. When Jim Watson launched the Human Genome Project
in 1989 and established the Working Group on Ethical, Legal, and
Social Implications of the Project, ELSI initially proved relatively
uncontroversial. Whether this venture was an expression of genu-

ine concern or only a case of scientists trying to protect their backs, it is still true that the incorporation of an ethical component into a high-profile scientific project symbolized a change in attitudes. Yet tensions remain; the difficult interactions of the ELSI Working Group with genome scientists reveal basic conflicts that interfere with progress in the application of ethics to science.

The genetics community has also faced up to the forgotten history of the eugenics movement. This history is now consistently raised in discussions about the implications of contemporary genetics. The Cold Spring Harbor Laboratory on Long Island, currently a center of molecular biology and cancer research, but once the home of the Eugenics Records Office, has recently opened up its archives. Its website provides a valuable detailed account of the eugenics movement, and displays original documents. Historians of science who are specialists in the eugenics era act as consultants and provide commentary for the website.

I have also seen increasing student interest in exploring social responsibility in science. In 1987, two graduate students in the biology program at the Harvard Medical School came to ask for my help. They were unhappy that their curriculum did not deal with the social impact of science and wanted me to work with them to organize a course on the subject. Together, we developed an outline for a course that we called Social Issues in Biology; it would begin with the philosophy and history of science as background, then tackle contemporary concerns such as genetic screening, the status of women in science, issues involving race and genetics, and media coverage of science. It was I who worried that we wouldn't attract enough students, given an environment in which many faculty members let it be known that their students' attention should be focused exclusively on their science. It was the students who assured me that there would be interest in such a course. They were right; we attracted students whose numbers have grown over the

for his role as a founding member of the Dada movement in Zurich in 1916, later became a psychoanalyst in New York. In his autobiography *Memoirs of a Dada Drummer*, he describes why, after thirty years, he left a profession that stifled his revolutionary spirit. In the late 1960s at the age of seventy-seven he returned to Europe:

> I wanted to be a hippie again, a dadaist hippie in my own style with short hair and a good suit but a hippie anyway. My desire to be disorderly, chaotic and malfunctioning, although constantly thwarted by the AMA [American Medical Association] and my colleagues, became overwhelming.

The other was from an obituary for Dr. Harland Wood, an eminent American microbiologist, who died at the age of eighty-four.

> During the last weeks of his life as he fought the lymphoma that was steadily taking its toll on his energies, Harland Wood stayed in continual contact with his laboratory, checking on the details of experiments planned for that week. On the day before his death he received the good news, while in the hospital, that one of the manuscripts he had been revising had been accepted for publication in the *Journal of Biological Chemistry*.

Which way to go? Continue doing science to the very end, devote myself entirely to social activism, or explore my other nonscientific passions? Was there really a conflict? The answer rose to the surface of my consciousness in a strange transformatory moment—a moment that helped reconcile these warring tendencies. It happened about fifteen years ago. I was in the library of our department reading through the latest scientific journals. I came across an elegant scientific report, not extraordinary, but just a very satisfying piece of science. As I finished the article, I said to myself aloud, "I really love this stuff. I love science." I had never explicitly expressed that thought before. At that moment, I saw that I had loved science for a very long time, but had never fully recognized it. I have come to love it more and more.

In an early chapter I described the lecture given by Art Pardee to one of his students in Berkeley in 1961, comparing scientists to hot-air balloons that either rise or fall. I began to worry that I would be the next recipient of this metaphoric lesson on commitment to science. After Art moved his lab to Princeton, I did receive the equivalent of that lecture, albeit in a different form. "You know, Jon," he told me, "if you don't drop some of these outside activities—readings over the radio, singing in madrigal groups, and the like—you'll never win the Nobel Prize." Well, I may not have won the Nobel Prize, but the balloon has risen, sandbags and all. My sandbags may even have helped.

Today my excitement about my lab's research is stronger than ever. I am no longer conflicted; I no longer dream of other lives. I feel more committed than ever to communicating the joy of doing science and to explaining its method as an important way of thinking about problems. But at the same time I know that scientists as well as the public need to do a better job of understanding the limitations of science and the effects of society on its practice. Some scientists, such as Jacques Monod and C. P. Snow, have argued that inherent in science are fundamental "ethical" or "moral" principles that provide a basis for society's ethics. I love what we scientists do enough to believe that science does have something to offer in this regard, but I prefer less hubris about the powers of science. We should be more humble about what science is and is not capable of, not overselling its objectivity and proclaiming it as the solution to society's problems. We should heed the wisely restrained words of my scientific hero François Jacob: "science cannot answer all questions. It can, however, give some indications, exclude certain hypotheses. Engaging in the pursuit of science may help us make fewer mistakes. It's a sort of gamble." That is enough to satisfy me.

Bibliography

1 ▲ The Quail Farmer and the Scientist

Isenberg, S. 2001. *A Hero of Our Own: The Story of Varian Fry.* New York: Random House.

2 ▲ Becoming a Scientist

Beckwith, J. R. 1964. "A deletion analysis of the *lac* operator region in E. coli." *Journal of Molecular Biology* 8:427–430.

Beckwith, J. R., E. R. Signer, and W. Epstein. 1966. "Transposition of the *lac* region of E. coli." *Cold Spring Harbor Symposium on Quantitative Biology* 31:393–401.

Judson, H. F. 1979. *The Eighth Day of Creation.* New York: Simon and Schuster.

Pardee, A. B., F. Jacob, and J. Monod. 1959. "The genetic control and cytoplasmic expression of 'inducibility" in the synthesis of β-galactosidase by E. coli." *Journal of Molecular Biology* 1:165–178.

Shapiro, J., L. MacHattie, L. Eron, G. Ihler, K. Ippen, and J. Beckwith. 1969. "The isolation of pure *lac* operon DNA." *Nature* 224:768–774.

Watson, J. D. 2001. *The Double Helix: A Personal Account of the Discovery of the Structure of DNA.* New York: Touchstone Books.

Weiner, C. 1999. "Social responsibility in genetic engineering: historical perspectives." In *Gene Therapy and Ethics*, ed. A. Nordgren, pp. 51–64. Uppsala: Acta Universitatis Uppsaliensis.

3 ▲ Becoming an Activist

Beckwith, J. 1986. "The radical science movement in the United States." *Monthly Review* 38(3):118–128.

Krimsky, S. 1982. *Genetic Alchemy: The Social History of the Recombinant DNA Controversy.* Cambridge: MIT Press.

Lear, J. 1978. *Recombinant DNA: The Untold Story.* New York: Crown.

Moore, K. 1996. "Organizing integrity: American science and the creation of public interest organizations, 1955–1975." *American Journal of Sociology* 101:1592–1627.

Moore, K., and N. Hala. 2002. "Organizing identity: the creation of Science for the People." In *Social Structure and Organizations Revisited*, ed. M. Ventresca and M. Lounsbury. New York: Elsevier (in press).

Snow, C. P. 1959. *The Two Cultures and the Scientific Revolution.* New York: Cambridge University Press.

4 ▲ On Which Side Are the Angels?

Beckwith, J. R. 1970. "Gene expression in bacteria and some concerns about the misuse of science." *Bacteriological Reviews* 34:222–227.

5 ▲ The Tarantella of the Living

Acton, H. 1998. *The Bourbons of Naples.* London: Prion.

6 ▲ Does Science Take a Back Seat to Politics?

Beckwith, J. 1986. "The radical science movement in the United States." *Monthly Review* 38(3):118–128.

Jacob, F. 1998. Of Flies, Mice, and Men. Cambridge: Harvard University Press.

7 ▲ Their Own Atomic History

Allen, G. 1975. "Genetics, eugenics, and class struggle." *Genetics* 79:29–45.

Baur, E., E. Fischer, and F. Lenz. 1931. *Human Heredity*. New York: MacMillan.

Chase, A. 1977. *The Legacy of Malthus: The Social Costs of Scientific Racism*. New York: Knopf.

Kevles, D. 1985. *In the Name of Eugenics: Genetics and the Uses of Human Heredity*. Berkeley: University of California Press.

Kühl, S. 1994. *The Nazi Connection: Eugenics, American Racism, and German National Socialism*. New York: Oxford University Press.

Larson, E. J. 1995. *Sex, Race, and Science: Eugenics in the Deep South*. Baltimore: Johns Hopkins University Press.

Ludmerer, K. 1972. *Genetics and American Society*. Baltimore: Johns Hopkins University Press.

Müller-Hill, B. 1998. "Human genetics and the mass murder of Jews, Gypsies, and others." In *The Holocaust and History: The Known, the Unknown, and the Reexamined*, ed. M. Berenbaum and A. J. Peck, pp. 103–114. Bloomington: Indiana University Press.

———1998. *Murderous Science: Elimination by Scientific Selection of Jews, Gypsies, and Others in Germany, 1933–1945*. Cold Spring Harbor, N.Y.: Cold Spring Harbor Laboratory Press.

———1999. "The blood from Auschwitz and the silence of the scholars." *History of Philosophy and the Life Sciences* 21:331–365.

Waldinger, R. 1973. "The High Priests of Nature: Medicine in Germany, 1883–1933." B.A. thesis, Harvard University.

8 ▲ The Myth of the Criminal Chromosome

Beckwith, J., and J. King. 1974. "The XYY syndrome: a dangerous myth." *New Scientist* 64:474–476.

Borgaonkar, D. S., and S. A. Shah. 1974. "The XYY chromosome male—or syndrome." *Progress in Medical Genetics* 10:135–222.

Brunner, H. G., M. Nelen, X. O. Breakefield, H. H. Ropers, and B. A. van Oost. 1993. "Abnormal behavior associated with a point mutation in the structural gene for monoamine oxidase A." *Science* 262:578–583.

Engel, E. 1972. "The making of an XYY." *American Journal of Mental Deficiency Research* 77:123–127.

Freedman, A. M., H. I. Kaplan, and W. I. Sadock. 1972. *Modern Synopsis of Comprehensive Textbook of Psychiatry.* Baltimore: William and Wilkins.

Goddard, H. H. 1912. *The Kallikak Family: A Study of the Heredity of Feeble-mindedness.* New York: Macmillan.

Jacobs, P. A. 1982. "The William Allan Memorial Award Address: human population cytogenetics: the first twenty-five years." *American Journal of Human Genetics* 34:689-698.

Jacobs, P. A., M. Brunton, M. M. Melville, R. P. Brittain, and W. F. McClemont. 1965. "Aggressive behavior, mental subnormality, and the XYY male." *Nature* 208:1351–1352.

Pyeritz, R., H. Schreier, C. Madansky, L. Miller, and J. Beckwith. 1977. "The XYY male: the making of a myth." In *Biology as a Social Weapon,* ed. Ann Arbor Science for the People, pp. 86–100. Minnneapolis: Burgess.

Suzuki, D., and Knudson, P. 1988. *Genethics: The Ethics of Engineering Life.* Toronto: Stoddart.

Witkin, H. A., S. A. Mednick, F. Schulsinger, E. Bakkestrom, K. O. Christiansen, D. R. Goodenough, K. Rubin, and M. Stocking. 1976. "Criminality in XYY and XXY men." *Science* 193:547–555.

9 ▲ It's the Devil in Your DNA

Allen, E., B. Beckwith, J. Beckwith, S. Chorover, D. Culver, M. Duncan, S. Gould, R. Hubbard, H. Inouye, A. Leeds, R. Lewontin, C. Madansky, L. Miller, R. Pyeritz, M. Rosenthal, and H. Schreier. 1975. "Against 'Sociobiology.'" *New York Review of Books,* November 13, pp. 182, 184–186.

Barash, D. P. 1977. *Sociobiology and Behavior.* New York: Elsevier.

Beckwith, B. 1984. "He-man, she-woman: *Playboy* and *Cosmo* groove on genes. *Columbia Journalism Review* February:46–47.

Beckwith, J. 1981. "The political uses of sociobiology in the United States and Europe." *The Philosophical Forum* 13:311–321.

Caplan, A. L. 1978. *The Sociobiology Debate*. New York: Harper & Row.

Chagnon, N. A. 1968. *Yanomamö: The Fierce People*. New York: Holt, Rinehart, and Winston.

Education Development Center. 1973. *Exploring Human Nature*. Cambridge: EDC.

Freeman, D. 1983. *Margaret Mead and Samoa: The Making and Unmaking of an Anthropological Myth*. Cambridge: Harvard University Press.

Hrdy, S. *The Woman That Never Evolved*. Cambridge: Harvard University Press.

Kitcher, P. 1985. *Vaulting Ambition: Sociobiology and the Quest for Human Nature*. Cambridge: MIT Press.

Sociobiology Study Group. 1984. *Biology as Destiny: Scientific Fact or Social Bias?* Cambridge: Science for the People.

Tierney, P. 2000. *Darkness in El Dorado: How Historians and Journalists Devastated the Amazon*. New York: W. W. Norton.

Wilson, E. O. 1975. *Sociobiology: The New Synthesis*. Cambridge: Harvard University Press.

———1978. *On Human Nature*. Cambridge: Harvard University Press.

10 ▲ I'm Not Very Scary Anymore

Beckwith, B. 1999. "Quicksand? Don't sink, just 'dance' over it." *Smithsonian*, November, p. 164.

Beckwith, J. 1995. "Villains and heroes in the culture of science." *American Scientist* 83:510–513.

Beckwith, J., and J. S. Alper. 1998. "Reconsidering genetic antidiscrimination legislation." *Journal of Law, Medicine, and Ethics* 26:205–210.

Billings, P. R., M. A. Kohn, M. deCuevas, J. Beckwith, J. S. Alper, and M. R. Natowicz. 1992. "Discrimination as a consequence of genetic testing." *American Journal of Human Genetics* 50:476–482.

Cook-Deegan, R. 1994. *The Gene Wars: Science, Politics, and the Human Genome*. New York: Norton.

Geller, L. N., J. S. Alper, P. R. Billings, C. I. Barash, J. Beckwith, and M. R. Natowicz. 1996. "Individual, family, and societal dimensions of genetic discrimination: a case study analysis." *Science and Engineering Ethics* 2:71–88.

Hall, S. S. 1990. "James Watson and the search for biology's 'Holy Grail.'" *Smithsonian*, February, pp. 41–49.

Müller-Hill, B. 1987. "Genetics after Auschwitz." *Holocaust and Genocide Studies* 2:3–20.

Rosenfeld, A. 1980. "Sociobiology stirs controversy over limits of science." *Smithsonian*, September, pp. 73–80.

Suzuki, D. 1987. *Metamorphosis: Stages in a Life.* Toronto: Stoddart.

Wexler, A. 1987. *Mapping Fate: A Memoir of Family, Risk, and Genetic Research.* Berkeley: University of California Press.

11 ▲ Story-Telling in Science

Bardwell, J. C. A., K. McGovern, and J. Beckwith. 1991. "Identification of a protein required for disulfide bond formation in vivo." *Cell* 67:581–589.

Derman, A. I., and J. Beckwith. 1991. "*Escherichia coli* alkaline phosphatase fails to acquire disulfide bonds when retained in the cytoplasm." *Journal of Bacteriology* 173:7719–7722.

Edgar, R. S. 1966. "Conditional lethals." In *Phage and the Origins of Molecular Biology*, ed. J. Cairns, G. S. Stent, and J. D. Watson. Cold Spring Harbor, N.Y.: Cold Spring Harbor Laboratory of Quantitative Biology.

Emr, S., M. Schwartz, and T. J. Silhavy. 1978. "Mutations altering the cellular location of the lambda receptor: an *Escherichia coli* outer membrane protein." *Proceedings of the National Academy of Sciences, U.S.A.* 75:5802–5606.

Jacob, F. 1988. *The Statue Within.* New York: Basic Books.

Judson, H. F. 1979. *The Eighth Day of Creation.* New York: Simon and Schuster.

Kolata, G. 1994. "Selling growth drug for children: the legal and ethical questions." *New York Times*, August 15, p. 1.

Michaelis, S., H. Inouye, D. Oliver, and J. Beckwith. 1983. "Mutations that alter the signal sequence of alkaline phosphatase in *Escherichia coli.*" *Journal of Bacteriology* 154:366–374.

Oliver, D. B., and J. Beckwith. 1981. "E. coli mutant pleiotropically defective in the export of secreted proteins." *Cell* 25:2765–2772.

Tian, H. P., D. Boyd, and J. Beckwith. 2000. "A mutant hunt for defects in membrane protein assembly yields mutations affecting the bacterial signal recognition particle and Sec machinery." *Proceedings of the National Academy of Sciences, U.S.A.* 97:4730–4735.

12 ▲ Geneticists and the Two Cultures

Allen, A., B. Anderson, L. Andrews, J. Beckwith, J. Bowman, R. Cook-Deegan, D. Cox, T. Duster, R. Eisenberg, B. Fine, N. Holtzman, P. King, P. Kitcher, J. McInerney, V. McKusick, J. Mulvihill, J. Murray, R. Murray, T. Murray, D. Nelkin, R. Rapp, M. Saxton, and N. Wexler. 1996. "The Bell Curve: statement by the NIH-DOE Joint Working Group on the Ethical, Legal, and Social Implications of Human Genome Research." *American Journal of Human Genetics* 59:487–488.

Andrews, L. B. 1999. *The Clone Age: Adventures in the New World of Reproductive Technology.* New York: Henry Holt.

Andrews, L. B., J. E. Fullarton, N. A. Holtzman, and A. G. Motulsky. 1994. *Assessing Genetic Risks: Implications for Health and Social Policy.* Washington, D.C.: National Academy Press.

J. Alper, C. Ard, A. Asch, J. Beckwith, P. Conrad, and L. N. Geller, eds. 2002. *The Double-Edged Helix: Social Implications of Genetics in a Diverse Society.* Baltimore: Johns Hopkins University Press.

Beckwith, J. 1997. "The responsibilities of scientists in the genetic and race controversies." In *Plain Talk about the Human Genome Project,* ed. E. Smith and W. Sapp, pp. 83–94. Tuskegee: Tuskegee University Press.

Bowman, J. E., and R. F. Murray. 1990. *Genetic Variation and Disorders of Peoples of African Origin.* Baltimore: Johns Hopkins University Press.

Burnett, D. G. 1999. "A view from the bridge: the two cultures debate, its legacy, and the history of science." *Daedalus* 128(2):193–218.

Cook-Deegan, R. 1994. *The Gene Wars: Science, Politics, and the Human Genome.* New York: Norton.

Gross, P. R., and N. Levitt. 1994. *Higher Superstition. The Academic Left and Its Quarrels with Science.* Baltimore: Johns Hopkins University Press.

Hacking, I. 1999. *The Social Construction of What?* Cambridge: Harvard University Press.

Herrnstein, R. J., and C. Murray. 1994. *The Bell Curve.* New York: Free Press.

Juengst, E. 1996. "Self-critical federal science? The ethics experiment within the U.S. Human Genome Project." *Social Philosophy and Policy* 13:66–95.

Labinger, J. A., and H. Collins. 2001. *The One Culture: A Conversation about Science.* Chicago: University of Chicago Press.

McKusick, V. A. 1998. *Mendelian Inheritance in Man: A Catalog of Human Genes and Genetic Disorders.* 12th ed. Baltimore: Johns Hopkins University Press.

Miller, D. 1999. "Being an absolute skeptic." *Science* 284:1625–1626.

Monod, J. 1971. *Chance and Necessity.* New York: Knopf.

NIH/DOE Working Group on Ethical, Legal, and Social Implications of Human Genome Research. 1993. "Genetic information and health insurance." *Human Gene Therapy* 4:789–808.

Sokal, A. 1996. "Transgressing the boundaries: toward a transformative hermeneutics of quantum gravity." *Social Text* 46/47:217–252.

Snow, C. P. 1998. *The Two Cultures and the Scientific Revolution.* New York: Cambridge University Press.

Trilling, L. 2000. *The Moral Obligation to Be Intelligent.* New York: Farrar, Straus & Giroux.

13 ▲ The Scientist and the Quail Farmer

Beckwith, B., and J. Beckwith. 2001. "Detectives of the desert: tracking Indian rock art is an art in itself." In *Travelers' Tales of the Southwest,* ed. S. O'Reilly and T. O'Reilly, pp. 181–190. San Francisco: Travelers' Tales.

Cold Spring Harbor Laboratory. "Image archive on the American Eugenics Movement." Available at http://vector.cshl.org/eugenics

Huelsenbeck, R. 1991. *Memoirs of a Dada Drummer.* Berkeley: University of California Press.

Jacob, F. 1998. *Of Flies, Mice, and Men.* Cambridge: Harvard University Press.

▲ ▲ ▲

Acknowledgments

Several people are responsible for making this book happen. First, my wife, Barbara, herself a writer and an activist in the National Writers' Union, has encouraged me for a long time to write such a book. Barbara was also my primary editor, going through my drafts and making extensive suggestions about both style and content. Because we had cowritten several articles together in the past, it was easy for me to see her points and make the necessary changes. Second, Misia Landau, an anthropologist and a senior science writer for the Harvard Medical Area Newsletter, *Focus*, planted the idea for this project at Harvard University Press. Third, my editor at the press, Michael Fisher, who invited me to prepare a proposal, guided me through several drastic changes in the structure and approach of the book. His ideas about possible ways to organize the material were absolutely essential for finally leading me to a format that worked. His editorial suggestions, during this process, were right on the mark. I thank Nancy Clemente for doing a remarkably thorough job of copy-editing and in rapid fashion, when I asked that it be done before my spring semester teaching started.

One of the pleasures of preparing the book was going back to old friends and acquaintances to check my memory of facts and events. These include Rita Arditti, Victor Brogna, Eric Juengst, Hal Peterson, Paul Primakoff, Jim Shapiro, Art Sussman, and Michael Yesley. I thank Joseph Alper, Paolo Bazzicalupo, and my sister Gail Mazur for reading chapters of the book and giving me feedback. I thank also the people in my lab for their patience, as I struggled to combine my writing effort with running a scientific laboratory. I particularly thank Federico Katzen, a postdoctoral fellow working with me, who graciously offered to prepare the figures after I gave up trying to learn the graphics program CorelDraw. My colleagues in the Genetic Screening Study Group have also been a constant source of support for my continuing in this double life I lead.

Thanks to the journal *Nature* for permission to reprint pictures and figures from the 1969 paper "The Isolation of Pure *lac* Operon DNA" and to the photographers Peter Menzel and Peter Simon for permission to reprint their photographs from *Smithsonian*.

Finally, I owe much to François Williams and our 1998 meeting in Normandy. This often emotional experience provided some of the impetus for looking at my careers in science and science activism in a larger perspective.

Index